Thought Experiments

Thought Experiments

History and Applications for Education

Chris Edwards

ROWMAN & LITTLEFIELD
Lanham • Boulder • New York • London

Published by Rowman & Littlefield
A wholly owned subsidiary of The Rowman & Littlefield Publishing Group, Inc.
4501 Forbes Boulevard, Suite 200, Lanham, Maryland 20706
www.rowman.com

British Library Cataloguing in Publication Information Available
Library of Congress Cataloging-in-Publication Data
Names: Edwards, Chris, 1977- author.
Title: Thought experiments : history and applications for education / Chris
    Edwards.
Description: Lanham, Maryland : Rowman & Littlefield, 2021. | Includes
    bibliographical references. | Summary: "Thought experiments do not
    require a laboratory and need no funding, yet they are responsible for
    several major intellectual revolutions throughout history. Given their
    importance, and the way that they immediately engage students, it is
    surprising that thought experiments are not used more frequently as
    teaching tools in the academic disciplines. Thought Experiments: History
    and Applications for Education explains how thought experiments
    developed and shows how thought experiments can be applied to subjects
    as varied as theoretical physics, mathematics, politics, personal
    identity, and ethics. Teachers at all levels and in all disciplines will
    discover how to use thought experiments effectively in their own
    classrooms"-- Provided by publisher.
Identifiers: LCCN 2020053445 (print) | LCCN 2020053446 (ebook) | ISBN
    9781475860740 (cloth) | ISBN 9781475860757 (paperback) | ISBN
    9781475860764 (epub)
Subjects: LCSH: Thought experiments. | Critical thinking--Study and
    teaching.
Classification: LCC BD265 .E48 2021 (print) | LCC BD265 (ebook) | DDC
    100--dc23
LC record available at https://lccn.loc.gov/2020053445
LC ebook record available at https://lccn.loc.gov/2020053446

Contents

Introduction

A thought experiment is an experiment that exists purely in the mind It differs in purpose from a scientific experiment because the object is to clarify analogical reasoning rather than to collect experimental evidence. The scientific community does not scoff at thought experiments, but rather treats them as being occasionally useful for clarification. Some of these experiments, partially through their flashy names, are now embedded in the intellectual lexicon. "The Trolley Problem" and "The Prisoner's Dilemma" get used quite a lot in ethics and economics. Yet the thought experiment remains underused. As I hope to prove in this book, thought experiments, when framed by scientific principles and shaped by logic, can clear up much of the confusion in what may broadly be conceived of as the problems inherent in the entire modern conception of knowledge and theories about knowledge.

My own attraction to thought experiments comes from happy moments of reading and private contemplation. Thought experiments simply come with less hassle than scientific experiments; I often find that experiments made of thought obsess my mind regardless of their importance or triviality. Often, it turns out that a trivial thought experiment turns out to be transferrable to a more important problem. Few things are more pleasing to the intellect than the act of developing a symmetrical analogy between two scenarios.

For example, my sons and I enjoy watching the "World's Strongest Man" competitions that air frequently on ESPN 2. Watching giants hoist boulders of various sizes onto platforms and tow semis always forces the same question upon me: "Just how much stronger are these guys than I am?" The question obsesses me partially because powerlifting is such an enjoyable thing when done right, and I have found that I really need to have simple health-oriented goals (a nice way of saying I just like to have an hour of meathead time in my day) to focus on.

Nothing can be simpler than, say, the deadlift. When you see a bar with weights on the ground, you pick it up and then you put it back down. Even if someone were to complete part one, and then forget what to do, the second part will soon make itself apparent and he will naturally put the bar back down.

The question I developed, from both weightlifting and watching professional strongmen, was this: "Is a strongman to me what I am to a toddler?" Let's say, for example, that I can deadlift four hundred pounds and that a strongman can deadlift eight hundred (quite a few of them can lift more than this, but the symmetry of the analogy is nice). Does this mean that the difference in strength between me and a professional strongman is just about the same as the difference in strength between myself and a toddler who can deadlift only one pound?

This can't be. For one thing, even though I despise mixed martial arts (more on that in a later chapter), I have seen incredibly strong powerlifters be easily beaten up by professional fighters who are probably about my size and who can probably lift a similar amount to me. (Disclaimer: this in no way indicates that I personally would ever want to tussle with any of the strongman competitors; I am merely pointing this out to establish a problem with my toddler analogy). A toddler could never muster the strength to do any kind of damage at all to any grown man my size.

So, what is the proper way to think of my hypothetical strength level, via analogy, to a professional strongman? Well, let's make this a proper analogy: Lifter A can deadlift one pound. Lifter B can deadlift four hundred pounds. Lifter C can deadlift eight hundred pounds. (To connect to the given scenario, A, B, and C correspond to the toddler, me, and a professional strongman.) For a number of reasons, it seems wrong to think that Lifter C is to Lifter B what Lifter B is to Lifter A. So there must be something wrong with the comparative analogy. What's the right analogy, then?

Let's think of the eight hundred pounds as a pile of weight. It takes Lifter C only one trip to move the pile. It takes Lifter B two trips, and it takes Lifter A eight hundred trips. Given this analogy, lifter B and C are actually closer to each other in their strength levels when compared to Lifter A. This seems to reflect reality better than to declare that Lifter C is to Lifter B what Lifter B is to Lifter A. (And it salves the ego of an intermediate-level lifter a bit.)

At this point, you may be asking the question that all philosophers dread: "Who cares?" I agree, this seems like a pointless mental exercise. Yet, the reasoning can now be transferred to levels of wealth and poverty. Let's look at this similar question: "Is Bill Gates to me what I am to a deeply impoverished child in India?" As was the case with the weightlifters/toddler analogy, the answer is no. To explain why, consider this paragraph from Steven Pinker's *Enlightenment Now: The Case for Reason, Science, Humanism, and Progress* (2018):

> Together, technology and globalization have transformed what it means to be a poor person, at least in developed countries. The old stereotype of poverty was an emaciated pauper in rags. Today, the poor are likely to be as overweight as their employers, and dressed in the same fleece, sneakers, and jeans. The poor used to be called have-nots. In 2011, more than 95 percent of American households below the poverty line had electricity, running water, flush toilets, a refrigerator, a stove, and a color TV. (A century and a half before, the Rothschilds, Astors, and Vanderbilts had none of these things.) Almost half of the households below the poverty line had a dishwasher, 60 percent had a computer, around two-thirds had a washing machine and a clothes dryer, and more than 80 percent had an air conditioner, a video recorder, and a cell phone (p. 119).

Earlier in his book, Pinker conjured up this thought experiment, phrased as a question:

> A refrigerator today costs around $500. How much would someone have to pay you to give up refrigeration? Surely far more than $500! Adam Smith called it the paradox of value: when an important good becomes plentiful, it costs far less than people are willing to pay for it (p. 82).

Given that type of question, we can now ask how much it would cost for me to give up all of the things that I have that a poor child in India lacks: flush toilets, clean running water, a coffeemaker, washer and drier, two cars, a yard, vaccinations, dental care, etc. I would not take any amount of money to give all of these up, especially not vaccinations, but even if we assume that I would take $10 million to give up using refrigeration in any way, then we can assume that I currently live a life that is materially superior to anyone who possessed $10 million in 1940, and therefore live a life that is substantially superior to a poor Indian child today.

From the child's perspective, the actual value of what I own puts me very close in lifestyle to Bill Gates and Mark Zuckerburg. In the modern United States, just about anyone can travel cheaply on a commercial airline, but we feel less than wealthy because some people own private jets.

These are two simple thought experiments and they are not trivial. When I see a strongman who can deadlift eight hundred pounds, I no longer feel so inferior. I think, "Well, it takes him one trip to move a weight that it would take me two trips to move." When I hear politicians attacking the "one percent," I take a moment to realize that, in terms of absolute value, I (a high school teacher, no less) am one of the wealthiest human beings to ever exist. In the 1980s, President Reagan used to screen films in a private theater at the White House on a movie reel. I can call up just about any movie ever made at any time and watch it on a handheld device without wires.

This perspective matters because it changes the way that we think, and the way we think determines how we interact with each other, how we vote, and how we interact with things like society, education, equality, and, especially, epistemology. Scientific experiments exist to collect research data; thought experiments exist to help us collect our thoughts and correct our perceptions.

Readers might expect a section on Albert Einstein's famous thought experiments regarding motion and light, but the Einstein industry being what it is, Einstein's approaches to philosophy and science are well-known enough that they need not be rehashed here. Besides, John Gribbin covered Einstein's thought processes as well as anybody possibly could in his book *Einstein's Masterwork: 1915 and the General Theory of Relativity* (2015). I reviewed that work for *Skeptic* magazine and will make references to Einstein's thought processes when necessary for the purpose of helping to explain other ideas, but will not give them specific placement in this book.

Parts of this book will be based on papers that I have written for *Skeptic* magazine. *Skeptic* is a premier science and philosophy journal, and I have been honored to have had multiple papers published in it; my hope is that readers of this book will appreciate that some of the more complex forms of reasoning have been peer reviewed and published in a journal. None of the previous papers will be recreated here entirely, but the reasoning from those papers will prove to be useful in the development of these thought experiments.

As a scholar and teacher, my interests are in the development of cross-curricular lessons and insights. Thought experiments function in a traditional philosophical sense by actually solving problems. However, they also, and probably more than any other teaching method, require students to think at a deep level in the subject of analogy. What is similar and what is different between cases? In addition, thought experiments always require students to study the situation in a metacognitive way, by challenging their own base assumptions involving the subjects at hand. Thought experiments might be the key in breaking away from the passing-on-of-received-knowledge-and-skills educational model that still dominates.

The layout of this book will be as follows: Chapter One will explore and analyze the most famous existing thought experiments. Chapter Two will explain how a thought experiment in time travel can clear up a great deal of confusion in physics. In Chapter Three, we will clear up the mathematical problems inherent with the concept of infinity and develop a thought experiment in analogies which will explain why the Big Bang is an unlikely source of the universe.

Having solved all the big problems using our thought experiments, we will then turn our attention to fixing American politics in Chapter Four. In Chapter Five, the power of thought experiments will lead us to a clear examination of how to analyze ethics involving risk and reward. Chapter Six will explore the concept of identity and self, and Chapter Seven will show how thought experiments can help create a new and effective form of ethical reasoning. Chapter Eight will explore the usage of meta-mathematics and meta-language in solving problems. That's probably enough for one book, and my hope is that by solving some of humanity's oldest problems, the importance of thought experiments will be made apparent and their usage will be expanded. The application to education will be included throughout, but it is my assertion that a good book of philosophy leaves the reader a little room to think on her own, so students, professionals, scholars, and teachers are invited to take from this what is useful and to experiment with their own thoughts.

Ultimately, a thought experiment has two useful purposes. The first is to clarify one's own thoughts and the second is for the purposes of teaching. The applications to education will be included at the end of each chapter and professors and teachers might use those applications to help create their own curricula, or use the questions directly should they choose to use this book as a core text.

KEY POINTS FOR EDUCATIONAL APPLICATION

- Thought experiments are different from traditional scientific experiments in the sense that a thought experiment does not exist for the purpose of collecting new evidence. The purpose of a thought experiment is to develop a proper analogy and to study a model through an epistemological viewpoint.
- Thought experiments can be developed for questions that are both mundane and profound. Frequently, a thought experiment as applied to a frivolous problem generates an insight that can be applied to a more meaningful problem.
- Thought experiments are valuable for just about every field and can be applied in a cross-curricular manner to solve older problems. Professors and teachers will find them to be a great way to engage students.

Chapter One

Famous Thought Experiments

Thought experiments come in different categories, and some experiments will overlap. Three of the most famous involve one involving the concept of a future "singularity," or point where the universe itself becomes conscious; the "Trolley Problem," which is a riddle of sorts that engages one's emotional and cognitive reasoning skills; and "The Prisoner's Dilemma," which is a construct of game theory and is tied to rational choice. Analyzing these three best-known thought experiments will help to provide logical consistency as we expand the concepts in subsequent chapters.

Ray Kurweil and the Singularity

The concept of a "singularity," established by the inventor and futurist Ray Kurzweil in his bestselling book, *The Singularity is Near: When Humans Transcend Biology* (2005), consists of the notion that humanity and technology intertwine to move history in a specific direction. Kurzweil imagines a scenario where current trends regarding technological complexity will continue until they reach an inevitable singularity point when the universe will "wake up."

Kurzweil's prediction cannot be described as new, but in order to analyze him and the flaws of his thought experiment, he must be compared to the right historical philosopher. It is tempting to compare the philosophy of Kurzweil with that of the Jesuit theologian Pierre Teilhard de Chardin (1881–1955), since both men noted that the evolution of humanity and society trends toward ever greater levels of complexity. Kurzweil's ideas about predicting the future are also similar to those of Karl Marx, who believed that by understanding history it becomes possible to predict an inevitable future outcome.

But, in fact, Kurzweil's philosophy is more analogous with that of St. Thomas Aquinas, who was commissioned by the Catholic Church in the 13th century to "prove" the tenets of Christianity using newly discovered Aristotelian logic. Aquinas, as Bertrand Russell pointed out, was not a true philosopher, since he already knew the conclusion and tried to blaze a trail of reason backwards. When this proved impossible, Aquinas could simply use faith as a crutch. Although different in form, this is the same flawed approach to a philosophical thought experiment that Kurzweil takes.

Before pointing out the errors of Kurzweil's thought experiment regarding a future "singularity," it is first necessary to encapsulate his theory: Kurzweil's major assertion is that human evolution should be divided into six epochs.

1. Epoch One involved *Physics and Chemistry*, which included the storing of information in atoms.
2. Epoch Two, titled *Biology*, included the transformation of matter into "life," and thus of physics into biology.
3. Epoch Three, titled *Brains*, involved the evolution of the human brain.
4. Epoch Four, called *Technology*, involved the creation of information and hardware systems. The first four epochs are interesting, and Kurzweil is outstanding at describing a process that has already occurred.
5. Epoch Five is the *Merger of Technology and Intelligence*, which Kurzweil describes like this: "The methods of biology (including human intelligence) are integrated into the (exponentially expanding) human technology base" (p. 15).
6. Epoch Six is even more dramatic, in that Kurzweil predicts that all of the particles of the universe will be endowed with data processing capabilities and will also be able to store knowledge. This is the point where the universe will "wake up." (Besides this, an awful lot of good things, including eternal life, are supposed to come to humanity in the future.)

Unfortunately this thought experiment, one where Kurzweil predicts and imagines the future, is built upon three major logical and scientific errors.

The icon of Kurzweil's techno-theology is the "S" curve, designed to show exponential growth in the power of technology. Kurzweil correctly sees technological evolution as being an extension of biological evolution, but does not take into account all of the aspects of this analogy.

In nature, complexity comes with an energy cost, so organisms don't become complex just for the sake of it. Simple organisms such as worms are as abundant as simple inventions such as ink pens because sometimes complexity isn't worth the energy and simplicity is good enough. Technology evolves to survive in the market, not to be complex, and if the cost is too great to supply a return, then the rate of complexity will slow down.

Exponential growth can slow, stop, or recede very quickly if the energy cost is too much. Flight, for example, did evolve rapidly between Kitty Hawk and the first moon landing, but the cost of deep space exploration is simply too great to justify (especially without the motivation provided by the Cold War), so manned flight complexity settled into jet travel.

Even at the pinnacle of that stage—the Supersonic Transport, or the Concorde—went into reverse due to economic and political restraints on the upward sloping curve. Even when humans made it to the moon, we were, practically speaking, no closer to landing people on Mars than we were before leaving Earth.

If evolutionary history moves in a direction, then why hasn't Epoch Six, where the universe "wakes up," already occurred in some alien civilization somewhere else in the universe? Here is Kurzweil's answer:

> The conclusion that I reach is that it is likely (although not certain) that there are no such other civilizations. In other words, we are in the lead. That's right, our humble civilization with its pickup trucks, fast food, and persistent conflicts (and computation!) is in the lead in terms of the creation of complexity and order in the universe. Now how can that be? Isn't this extremely unlikely, given the sheer number of likely inhabited planets? Indeed it is very unlikely, but equally unlikely is the existence of our universe, with its set law of physics and related physical constants, so exquisitely, precisely what is needed for the evolution of life to be possible, if the universe didn't allow the evolution of life we wouldn't be here to notice it. Yet here we are. So by a similar anthropic principle, we're here in the lead in the universe. Again, if it weren't here, we would not be noticing it (p. 357).

The anthropic principle cannot be used to favor a prediction, only to explain an event that has already occurred. If one adds enough factors, then the odds of perfectly ordinary events can be made to sound outlandishly low. For example, the odds on a Wednesday afternoon that the workers in a certain office will all show up wearing clothes on Thursday morning are pretty good.

However, if one tried to predict the color schemes and styles of those clothes (thus adding factors), the odds of being right would drop dramatically because of the large number of different possible combinations. After everyone shows up on Thursday morning, dressed in one of those heretofore incredibly unlikely combinations, then one can invoke the anthropic principle to explain this ordinary event.

But only after the fact. The workers had to be clothed in some possible combination, and this is how it randomly ended up. To simplify, I cannot buy a lottery ticket and say "By invocation of the anthropic principle, I will win." (Well, I could say it, but everybody in the 7/11 would probably give me strange looks.)

The future has to look some way, but not necessarily the way Kurzweil thinks it will. Just because the anthropic principle can be used to explain the occurrence of a highly unlikely event *post facto*, this emphatically does not mean that it can be used to confidently predict that a highly unlikely event will occur in the future.

Again, Kurzweil is reasoning in reverse, creating a syllogism that looks like this: A. The universe is destined to "wake up." B. The universe has not yet "woken up." C. Therefore, our civilization must be leading the charge.

The final problem with Kurzweil's thought experiment is more concrete. The speed of light isn't fast enough for the universe to wake up as quickly as he predicts. This constitutes a major issue, since Einstein's theory of relativity predicts that it is not possible for anything to accelerate to the speed of light.

Kurzweil, however, dismisses this fundamental rule of physics by simply claiming that it is possible to go faster than light in the sense that relativity theory does not forbid space from expanding faster than light (some models of the early universe state that this may have occurred after a "big bang"), although relativity theory does forbid information carrying particles from accelerating to that speed.

No matter, Kurzweil predicts that physicists will either figure out a way around light speed (maybe they can stop entropy while they are at it), or that humans will use wormholes as a detour. Why does he think this is possible?

> [L]imits are not always what they seem. New scientific understanding has a way of pushing apparent limits aside. As one of many such examples, early in the history of aviation, a consensus of analysis of the limits of jet propulsion apparently demonstrated that jet aircraft was infeasible (p. 138).

But sometimes limits are what they seem. The speed of light "barrier" is not like the "speed of sound" barrier. Physicists were perfectly aware of faster-than-sound particles well before the development of jets. Einstein's theory of relativity is itself a thought experiment, one wherein Einstein posited questions about the nature of motion and speed and then formed an analogy. Energy is like mass ($E = M$) and if we square the speed of light (C, for *celeritas*, which is Latin for "speed") then we create a square picture frame of theory that describes everything in the universe that moves slower than light speed. Had Einstein create $E = MS_2$ with the "S" standing for "sound," then he would have created a square picture frame of theory that describes everything in the universe that moves slower than the speed of sound.

Does this mean that Kurzweil could be right in saying that information could travel faster than the speed of light? Maybe. But this is not what Kurzweil's thought experiment proclaims. He states that modern human civilization on Earth will create this singularity, and that means he believes that we humans will develop means of accelerating particles past the speed of light; something beyond the limits of ordinary physical rules regarding acceleration and speed.

Kurzweil offers no detailed explanation, no coherent theory, for how this "limit" can be surpassed, but merely calls on the reader to put his or her faith into an ever-increasing power of technology and science. And faith, whether it be in gods, fairies, or technological advancement, is never useful in the scientific sense. Like Aquinas, Kurzweil already knows the ending, and in both worldviews there is eternal life waiting for those who believe.

The Trolley Problem and the Problem of Autocracy, or Self-Driving Cars

Imagine the following scenario: You are standing next to a fork in a railroad line where there is a switch. There are five workers on the one track and one worker on the other track. A trolley car is hurtling down the track and is about to hit and kill the five workers unless you throw the switch and divert the car down the other branch, thereby killing the one worker instead. Would you throw the switch to kill one worker in order to save five?

Most people say they would kill one worker in order to say five. In a second scenario, you are standing on a bridge next to a large man. The trolley is once again speeding down the track and is about to hit and kill five workers, unless you push the large man onto the track, killing him but stopping the car, thereby killing the one in order to save five. Would you throw the man? Most people say they would not.

This is a classic thought experiment first proposed in 1967 by the philosopher Phillipa Foot that has become ingrained into a hot new area of research called Moral Cognition Testing (MCT) which is being employed by psychologists and philosophers who study human behavior and brains in relation to morality. A 2011 *Discover* magazine article entitled "The End of Morality" by Kristin Ohlson, for example, profiled the work of Harvard scientists Joshua Greene and Fiery Cushman, who present people with a variety of such moral scenarios and then ask for responses.

For example: A runaway hot dog cart hurtles toward a group of bicyclists. Should you push the cart into the crowd, killing three people, or let the cart slam into some passing bicyclists, killing a dozen? Another scenario, which purportedly stumped Green in a high school debate and made him rethink his utilitarian philosophy, involves asking whether or not it would be moral to kill a single person and harvest his organs so that five people might live. Supposedly, both scenarios involve the same type of reasoning and involve the same outcomes so there is little moral difference.

There are two problems with the above dilemmas. To begin with, nothing in the real world operates in such a clean way with limited and perfectly predictable outcomes. I would not shove the hot dog cart into a crowd because it reduces a crucial component of the scenario: time.

In the real world, acting quickly in that situation reduces the probability that someone would scream and alert the riders or that one of the riders would see the cart and actually move. By shoving the cart, I've immediately caused the deaths of the bystanders. By reducing time, I've reduced the possibility of better outcomes. In reality, actions do not usually have such absolute endings, and presenting people with absolutes does not really help to ascertain how they reason morally.

For the second scenario, one should not kill the man and harvest his organs, and not do so for good utilitarian reasons. Killing the man may at first appear to be the best action for the most people, but in fact doing so would give moral justice to a concept that over time would create a great amount of fear and uncertainty that would eventually do more damage to more people.

If society considered it morally justifiable to kill people who were in waiting rooms, even for good reasons, then hospital visits would likely decline and human misery would increase. The scenarios involving hot dog carts and hospital visits are not similar because, while runaway wiener carts are likely singular events, hospital bystanders are common. One can't compare the two because the effects of action in the second scenario have larger societal outcomes.

More will be said about ethical thought experiments in a later chapter, but a few points should be stated here. The concept of "larger societal outcomes" remains underused by Utilitarian philosophers. An action that affects an individual negatively almost never turns out to be good for the group entirely.

Anti-utilitarian arguments sometimes take the form of "if four people were stranded on a desert island, it would be good for the group if one person was eaten by the other three." This would not be the case; even if one considers the inherent problems that would come with trying to prepare and eat a human corpse on a desert island. Presumably, none of the four would want to be eaten, so a general agreement that no one gets eaten might be seen as being for the greater good.

If we remove the scenario from the desert island, it's hard to find any conditions where three people deciding to eat one person would be beneficial for the group. This is true particularly if we start to consider the anxiety-inducing effects that the logic of cannibalism would have on the group. At some level, Utilitarian philosophy is an offshoot of Immanuel Kant's (1724–1804) famous "categorical imperative." Translations from the German vary, but Kant's philosophy can be paraphrased in question form as, "If my action was made a universal rule, would it be positive for humanity?"

The categorical imperative causes much moral confusion because, like the "I before E except after C" rule that children learn when they first encounter English grammar, it works well enough most of the time. Ethics, however, permits no universal rule, because the word "universal" remains open to interpretation.

For example, let's imagine an ethical English philosopher/soldier in a WWI trench with 20 of his comrades. Half a mile across from our soldier, 20 German soldiers sit crouched down in their own trench, weapons in hand. If our English soldier decides not to fight, and everyone in both trenches followed his example, this would work out well for everyone in true Kantian fashion.

However, if the philosopher/soldier decides not to fight and the Germans fail to be inspired by his ethics, then his action merely aided in the destruction of the other soldiers in his own trench. If "universal" gets defined by our soldier and the 19 other British soldiers in his trench, then deciding not to fight would be suicidal. If all 40 soldiers involved in this scenario decide not to fight, then everyone wins (until they are court-martialed, that is).

A variation of this problem with the categorical imperative is known as "the Prisoner's Dilemma," which will be the third great historical thought experiment explored in this chapter. Another Trolley-like problem, favored in the *Discover* article by Joshua Greene, involves a crying baby and some hypothetical soldiers. Imagine yourself in a room holding your hand over your baby daughter's mouth to prevent her from crying.

Evil soldiers are outside, hunting you and your family and friends. Should you remove your hand and let the baby breathe (and cry), or should you preserve the hiding place by smothering the baby? (This scenario was, in fact, played out in the final episode of the popular television series M*A*S*H.) Such a scenario is psychologically pointless in that it will not tell anyone how people morally reason, primarily because it removes a peer pressure dynamic.

For most people, the real answer to how they would react in such a scenario would likely be dramatically affected by the responses of the other people in the hiding place, and we cannot assume that all of those people would be selfishly interested in survival. Medieval Jews faced with homicidal Crusaders often committed mass ritual suicide, with group dynamics and pressure overriding the survival impulse.

Think of how quickly such role-playing becomes silly when you try to add additional peer pressure factors. Here are a couple of examples: 1. You are a Rwandan Tutsi surrounded by three family members and two strangers—one of the strangers wants you to smother the baby, the other one is paralyzed by fear and expresses no preference, and your family wants you to let the baby scream. Genocidal Hutus are just outside of your hiding place. What do you do? 2. You are a medieval Jew, raised in a family that places pride of religion first, etc. Since an ethicist cannot actually become another person with a separate identity; these questions of ethics become almost irrelevant.

Also, I shouldn't shove the man in front of a trolley because I can't do the calculations quickly enough to determine whether his weight would stop the trolley's momentum. By shoving him, I would most likely create a situation where the man died a messy death and everybody else still got maimed or killed. Besides, if I had enough time to shove the man, I could just as easily yell at the (apparently blind) folks hanging out on the trolley track.

Greene and Cushman, working with a neuroscientist from Princeton named Jonathan Cohen, are studying which parts of the brain become engaged when participants are asked to reason through such situations. Greene, Cushman, and Cohen then create scientific theories to explain the results. When it was found, for example, that only 30% of people would shove a hypothetical man in front of the hypothetical trolley but that 60% would pull a lever that would drop the man through a trapdoor onto the tracks, Greene noted: "We seem to have this general mechanism that makes us reluctant to engage in physical violence. . . . In this very unusual case, our emotions don't distinguish between gratuitous violence and acts aimed at promoting the general good."

Here Greene is theorizing over highly compromised facts based upon a hypothetical scenario with strictly defined outcomes. In effect, he's theorizing about real human behavior based on hypothetically controlled situations that are in fact impossible to predetermine.

As he notes: "It's been increasingly difficult to find a single theory that fits [moral reasoning]. My approach is to say, forget the overriding theory. Our moral judgments are sensitive to kooky things, like whether you're pushing someone with your hands or dropping him with a switch. There is no single moral faculty; there's just a dynamic interplay between top-down control processes and automatic emotional control in the brain."

This is highly problematic because Green is reasoning from outcomes based on scenarios with fixed outcomes. Logical thinking in the form of snap judgments can be made when the future is uncertain. In the real world, moral actions rarely, if ever, have such fixed outcomes. Instead, the human mind must quickly consider the probabilities of a given action in a given situation.

The mind evolved specifically to assess risk in chaotic environments, and is quite good at it. We cannot ask a mind that reasons through risk assessment to apply its evolved moral function to static situations and expect to create theories that genuinely explain human reasoning. Greene and Cushman are measuring how people think about hypotheticals, but are not assessing how people reason morally.

Further, such research suffers from the fallacy of the false dilemma, which occurs when someone is presented with a set of choices and is told that these are the only selections available. Skeptics are familiar with this fallacy when creationists insists that if: A. evolution cannot explain some mystery (yet), then B. creationism must be the explanation. In a different form, this fallacy plagues MCT, because participants are asked to moralize about actions that have fixed and predictable outcomes, which is not the way that people reason in a world filled with multiple potential outcomes and uncertainty.

The Prisoner's Dilemma

Of the six thought experiments detailed in this opening chapter, The Prisoner's Dilemma (PD) may be the most well-known. This is probably because the PD features a scenario in which acting in one's own self-interest can lead to a worse outcome for yourself. A disconnect exists between the intent and the outcome, and since the scenario factors in the decision-making processes of other people, the PD itself becomes a powerful thought experiment that can be used across a variety of thought experiments.

The concept behind the PD was developed in 1950 by two RAND scientists named Merrill Flood and Melvin Dresher. Later, a Canadian game theorist and mathematician named Albert W. Tucker gave the concept its distinctive title and included the factor of the prison sentences. The thought experiment includes two recently arrested criminals. They generally go by the titles of Prisoner A and Prisoner B, but let's call them Bill and Larry.

Imagine that Bill and Larry are arrested and then prevented from communicating. Three options emerge:

A. Bill snitches on Larry and Larry refuses to snitch on Bill. Bill will be set free and Larry will receive a three-year sentence. This also applies vice versa.

B. If both Bill and Larry stay quiet, they each will be given a lesser charge
    and will spend just one year in prison apiece.
C. If Bill and Larry both snitch on each other, then both of them will be
    given a two-year sentence.

The interesting point of the PD is that what is good for you depends upon the
unknown actions of another person. If Bill stays quiet, that's good for Larry,
but if Larry decides he does not care about what's good for Bill, then he will
snitch. The situation is such that snitching produces the best outcome, but
only if the other person remains quiet. When both snitch, both end up serving
a longer sentence than they would have if both had stayed quiet.

For all of its fame, the PD really cannot rate as a great thought experiment
because it relies on too few factors. To explain, let's imagine that Stanley
Milgram's (1933–1984) famous psychological experiments regarding authority never occurred. Let's frame Milgram's work as a thought experiment. If
we set the scenario, where the subject is being told to deliver electrical shocks
to a person (an actor, as it turns out) in another room just because an authority in a white lab coat told her to, in the hypothetical realm and titled it The
Subject's Dilemma, it would look like this:

> Subject A receives stress and guilt for delivering shocks but would receive no
> penalty for not delivering the shocks.

In this static environment, one would see no reason for delivering shocks at
all. Yet the actual experiments (depending on the interpretation of the data
sets) that involved humans and their behavior found that many of the subjects
would act irrationally. We all know that hypothetical models cannot predict
human behavior, but that may be because the models fail to include all of the
factors. Let's look again at our Subject's Dilemma:

> Subject A receives stress and guilt for delivering shocks but would feel as if she
> was "in trouble" with authority if she delivered no shocks.

This is suddenly different. Rather than suffering no penalty, the subject feels
the pain of standing up to authority, something that few people are comfortable with. One can only assume that, like anything else, one becomes better
at it with practice.

Likewise, the PD does not factor in that a criminal might suffer negative
consequences for snitching on his partner. If a criminal keeps his mouth shut
about a caper, and his partner sings on him, then the quiet criminal might be
out for a little revenge after his three year sentence ends. The concept of liv-

ing in fear, or of being considered a snitch, might alter how someone behaves in this kind of dilemma.

Let's compare the PD to another thought experiment. Let's imagine that a father one day receives a text message from two men who have kidnapped his ten-year-old daughter. The men demand that a ransom be paid to a certain account and that the father not contact the authorities. When the money is paid, the men will set the girl free in a public park.

The father might know that his kidnappers have no logical reason to set the girl free. If caught, the kidnappers would be guilty of multiple felonies already, and to leave the girl alive would be to risk being identified later. After they received the money, they would have no more use for the girl and, since they have the girl, the father really has nothing to bargain with. Should the father pay the money? Logically, no. But I would pay in this situation. Wouldn't you?

The reason that most of us would pay is similar to the statement in the introduction regarding Steve Pinker's theory about the value of refrigeration. The question is not "how much money does a refrigerator cost?" but, "how much money would it take for you to give up refrigeration?" In the kidnapping case, the father might surmise that his daughter has a slightly higher chance of surviving if the payment is made.

There might not be a good reason for thinking this, and the likeliest scenario is that the father loses both a great deal of money and his daughter, rather than just his daughter, but in this condition the money itself becomes worthless next to the small percentage bump that paying the money might give his daughter toward survival.

Did you see that the Kidnapping Dilemma is almost the same as the Prisoner's Dilemma? In the kidnapping dilemma the father can either A. Not pay money and virtually guarantee that his daughter dies, but he loses a daughter and not his money. B. Pay money and his daughter will still likely die, and he loses his daughter *and* his money.

Meanwhile, the kidnappers are faced with a dilemma as well. If they don't receive the money, then killing the girl would open them up to murder charges. If they do receive the money, then giving the girl back could potentially make them vulnerable. Either way, the decision they make will alert the media and cause a police search. The best situation for them would be to receive the money and then kill the girl. Thus, by making the payment, the father actually makes it more likely that his daughter will die. This is true, however, only if the kidnappers are entirely rational. Given that they are snatching ten-year-old girls, this hardly seems likely, and so the best decision would likely be to pay and hope.

This is a morbid thought experiment, but it highlights the fundamental problem with the Prisoner's Dilemma: no moral decision can be reduced to quantifiable factors like money or the length of a prison sentence. The Kidnapper's Dilemma engages your emotional reasoning at a deeper level than the Prisoner's Dilemma does, which is why the parallels between the situations probably went unnoticed at first glance.

If both of the criminals in the Prisoner's Dilemma were in the mafia, they both would get a status bump, including protection while in the penitentiary, for staying quiet (or so watching crime movies would have one believe). While "snitching" might help someone to avoid prison, it might also mean the abandonment of one's entire life in a witness relocation program. How does the dilemma look then?

The Singularity, the Trolley Problem, and the Prisoner's Dilemma all represent a type of thought experiment: extrapolating on the future, moral reasoning via analogy, and the ethical reasoning in a situation where the outcome is dependent upon the actions of another person or persons, respectively. All have analogs in the past and present, and a few words should be said about these in this first chapter because they help to provide clarity going forward.

Pascal's Wager

The French theologian and mathematician Blaise Pascal (1623–1662) was clearly undone by his desire to reconcile his logical mind with the Christianity he hoped to believe in. Unable to find any level of compatibility between faith and reason, Pascal devised a logical construct to help him believe. Paraphrased, it reads "Christianity may or may not be true. However, if it is true and I live as an unbeliever, I will burn in Hell for eternity. If it is not true, and I live as a believer, I will just die and cease to exist. Therefore, it is better to live as a believer."

Several problems probably just immediately manifested in your mind. What version of Christianity is the right one to believe in? What if God is Muslim or Zoroastrian? What if God really wants you to doubt rather than to have faith? Doesn't this wager posit a "trickster" God who waits to punish people for believing the wrong way and reward people for believing the right way? Pascal's Wager is just not very good logic, but philosophers who pick on it might do well to recognize that this is not the actual wager that most believer's make.

Clearly, Pascal created a False Dilemma in believing that he had an either/or choice between belief and non-belief. He failed to recognize a belief in God for what it is: evidence that one has not learned to reason properly. A skeptic who debates a theologian about the existence of a god might state that "we don't debate the existence of obvious things like the Sun or the Moon. The fact that the issue is being debated at all indicates that the existence of a god is not clear, and so the debate can only be about the existence of a god with a certain set of characteristics, the first of which is that this god does not want to provide clear evidence of her existence. This is an odd way for a deity to behave."

However, Pascal's Wager is not the bet that most believers make. When the death of a loved one occurs, it might make the grieving person feel better in the present to believe that a reunion will one day occur in the afterlife. What is interesting is that people often think that in order to believe in an afterlife, they must also believe in the entire set of religious doctrines that support the concept of the afterlife. This makes Pascal's Wager more reasonable; if someone believes, then she receives a temporary (and likely miniscule) amelioration of emotional pain.

At some level, Pascal's Wager, the Prisoner's Dilemma, and the Kidnapper's Dilemma all involve one party making decisions which are affected by the decisions of another silent party.

The Autocracy Problem, Artificial Intelligence, and Self-rule in Cars

As self-driving cars have become more likely, a new debate about ethics and Artificial Intelligence has created a modern thought experiment: If a car driven by AI has a motorcyclist on either side of it, with Motorcyclist On the Right (MOTR) wearing a helmet and Motorcyclist on the Left (MOTL) not wearing a helmet, and if the car is behind a semi and something falls off the back of the semi, then should the car swerve left or right? If the car swerves into the MOTR, then the odds of the motorcyclist living are better than if the car swerves into the MOTL. However, by swerving into the MOTR, the AI-driven car punishes someone for wearing a helmet.

The scenario, again, limits too many factors and contains too many inconsistencies. It's easiest to just list them.

- A properly-functioning AI would recognize probabilities and avoid situations such as this. The car would not be close enough behind a semi that could potentially drop a load, and it would slow down before finding itself contained in such a spot. By analogy, try to imagine that a young woman has an app that helps her to avoid dangerous parts of a city. The question is not, "What would the app do if she was trapped between a mugger and a ravenous pit bull?" but "How could the app possibly let her get into that situation to begin with?"

- The purpose of an AI-driven car would be to increase safe transportation. In that way, an AI car is analogous to a subway or to airline travel. People who ride motorcycles do so for entertainment more than for transportation. No one rides a motorcycle on a subway track, and there are no planes-for-pleasure that fly alongside commercial aircraft at top altitudes. It would make very little sense to have motorcycles on the road that are driven by humans with cars driven by AI. This posits a question: should motorcyclists and human drivers be given a lane of their own? If so, would this become a "death lane" where virtually all motor vehicle accidents would occur?

It might seem unfair to "go meta" on these scenarios by questioning their parameters, but if a thought experiment lacks logically consistent boundaries, then it fails to instruct at all. Accidents often happen when a series of events come together at a focal point, such as A. the sun is in a driver's eyes, B. a pedestrian has headphones on, and C. kids in the back of the car are misbehaving. A highly functioning AI would be able to pick up on at least a few of these and avoid entering into a scenario that would entangle all the factors.

Now, to answer the "so what?" question, the last point about a human-driver "death lane" does have an immediate analog in the current world.

Random violence (serial violence) is declining. Is this because cell phones make people safer due to the possibility of quick connection with the police and because bystanders or victims can record criminal activity? If so, does this mean that serial predators will look to prey upon people in areas like out-of-the-way nature parks or Amish communities where cell phone access is unlikely to protect a victim? Are we creating "wi-fi-less" death lanes without knowing it, and if so, what should we do about it?

The Watchmaker Thought Experiment

Kurzweil's singularity conceit, the Trolley Problem, and the Self-Driving Car problem all fall into a category of error that can be called the False Analogy. No analogy between scenarios will ever be exact; the purpose of analogizing is to determine the similarities and differences between scenarios. However, a False Analogy occurs when a philosopher makes the case that two dissimilar scenarios are, somehow, exactly alike.

Kurzweil compared jet travel to the speed of light and assumed an analogy of evolutionary exponential growth without recognizing that evolution is often constrained by energy costs. The Trolley Problem compares a runaway trolley with a hospital waiting room and, in the analysis, fails to factor in that runaway trolleys are unique while hospital waiting rooms are common, and that difference is why the ethical reasoning for both situations must be different.

False analogies can be enormously useful as intellectual tools because identifying the problems with a false analogy can frequently lead to the development of new insights that get closer to the reality of a natural function, thus making the analogy itself more practically useful. The most (in)famous false analogy was created by the theologian William Paley (1743–185), who posited that if he came across a watch, that logically meant there must be a watchmaker.

Charles Darwin (1809–1882) stayed in the same room at Cambridge University that Paley had once inhabited and found himself piqued by Paley's watchmaker analogy. Eventually, Darwin would realize that a complicated thing does not need a more complicated thing to have created it. In fact, to think that a watch just popped into existence fully formed, without any ancestors, is an absurd notion.

Evolutionary Theory has it that a watch would evolve, with humans acting as an environmental selector that chooses the most efficacious models for survival. Evolution provides proof for its process in the form of sundials, water clocks, and bell towers as ancestors of the watch.

To analyze the failures of Paley's analogy was to create a theory of devastating clarity, and, by analogy, something that can explain every single complex thing, natural or mechanical, in the universe. Evolutionary theorists, when debating Creationists, overexplain and allow themselves to get bogged down in details about viral phalanges and the like, but evolution is not hard to understand. Did PlayStation 4 come out before PlayStation 3? Were there no antecedents to your iPhone? Did the Creation Museum in Kentucky just pop, fully formed and without the help of blueprints based on previous models, into existence in a moment?

For educational purposes, this chapter indicates that a bad thought experiment is generally built upon a false or incomplete analogy. Analogies that are built upon too little evidence, or that are constructed without context, might lead to a though experiment that is improperly constructed. Content study and mastery, therefore, usually lead to the most appropriate thought experiments.

For educators, the act of highlighting the history of thought experiments creates the right conditions for students to engage in an analysis of how the intellectual ideas that make up a core curriculum developed in the first place. In some ways, the big ideas of history tended to begin with esoteric questions that a person with a cross-curricular background then answered by seeing novel connections between content. By processing thought experiments, students can also apply skepticism for the purpose of uncovering false arguments in logic.

Clearly, thought experiments are too powerful and useful to not be applied to some of the deepest problems in modern human society. With these parameters in mind; we can now employ increasingly powerful thought experiments to humanity's most vexing questions. We might as well begin with the concept of time.

KEY POINTS

- Ray Kurzweil is a futurist who developed an elaborate thought experiment where he extrapolated current trends into the future without considering the limiting factor of his analogy: the cost of energy. This is similar to the problem with William Paley's incomplete "watchmaker" analogy.
- The Prisoner's Dilemma may be the most famous thought experiment in the philosophical canon, but it assumes a scenario that is sanitized of the types of penalties that affect people in the real world, such as a fear of revenge.
- Other thought experiments, such as Pascal's Wager, are created in an intellectual vacuum where one idea (heaven) and its opposite (no heaven) are put up as being equally probable.
- Another recurrent problem in thought experiments is the development of false or highly unlikely scenarios. Self-driving cars, for example, will likely develop safety features that prevent them from entering into situations where there are high probabilities of an accident occurring.

Chapter Two

Time Travel

When considering any time-travel scenario, a favorite conceit for science fiction books and movies, one might ask an uncomfortable question: "If someone travels back to 1955, is it also 1955 on Saturn?" If so, how would the time-traveler know? Is it only necessary for time to be the way it was in 1955 based on the traveler's limited knowledge?

This is a silly question, but it highlights the problems with any time travel consideration, and understanding the problems can help to lead to solutions that clarify our understanding of time. This is the purpose of the thought experiment. I reviewed James Gleick's book *Time Travel: A History* in a 2017 issue of *Skeptic* (which was also published on eSkeptic (making it eternally available online if anyone is interested in reading the full review). Gleick was interested in the concept as a literary idea more than anything, but his work provides an important central narrative for understanding time travel and, therefore, the concept of time in our theoretical models.

In his book, Gleick indicates that the widespread use of trains made humans realize that their relationship to distance differed depending on speed—it was only a matter of thinking about time before someone realized that our relationship to time also differed depending on speed. (More on this in a moment.) In the 1960 film version of the H. G. Wells book *The Time Machine* (1895), wherein Rod Taylor plays the lead character, there is a scene where he sits in the machine while the seasons pass rapidly outside his house window. It looks very similar to the way that a landscape looks as it seems to whip by when one stares out the window of a train.

Gleick writes that Wells did not bother himself much with the physics, as "He was just trying to gin up a plausible-sounding plot device for a piece of fantastic story-telling" (p. 4). Yet it is possible to see how the creativity of both Wells and Einstein branched off from the same concepts.

A scientific concept of time travel originated with Wells, but philosophical and poetic musings about time and its effects preceded the great man. Gleick showcases an impressive collection of quotes about time from Tennyson, Poe, and LaPlace. The second chapter then highlights "time travel" as a pop culture phenomenon explored by Mr. Peabody, Mark Twain, and Woody Allen.

The point of the discussion appears to be that Wells' 1895 novel *The Time Machine* turned time travel into a mechanistic possibility when he moved beyond a concept from a Proustian work about a man who slept for a long time in a chair (a concept that Wells himself borrowed for a work titled *The Sleeper Awakes* that featured a man sleeping for a long time in a comfortable chair). "Machines improved upon magic armchairs," writes Gleick, and "by the last years of the nineteenth century, novel technology was impressing itself upon the culture" (p. 31).

The most interesting section of the book comes when Gleick tries to frame the idea of time and the future itself in the context of the Age of Exploration:

> No one bothered with the future in 1516. It was indistinguishable from the present. However, sailors were discovering remote places and strange peoples, so remote places served well for speculating authors spinning fantasies. . . . William Shakespeare, whose imagination seemed limitless, who traveled freely to magical isles and enchanted forests, did not—could not—imagine different times. The past and present are all the same to Shakespeare: mechanical clocks strike the hour in Caesar's Rome, and Cleopatra plays billiards (p. 35).

The idea of the future as a thing to strive for should be seen as intertwined with the concept of discovery and the evolution of the scientific method. After crediting Isaac Asimov with developing the idea of "futurism" as a concept denoting the imagining of a speculative time (as if the future was analogous to an island that one sailed to), Gleick then heaps some more importance on a well-known historical cause, that of the printing press. "It began in earnest with the Gutenberg printing press, saving our cultural memory in something visible, tangible, and shareable. It reached critical velocity with the Industrial Revolution and the rise of the machine—looms and mills and furnaces, coal and iron and steam—creating, along with so much else, a sudden nostalgia for the apparently vanishing agrarian way of life" (p. 41).

Was that it? Or was it that humans, in those early years of science and steam, simply did not know just exactly where the boundaries of scientific achievement could be drawn? Just a few decades before Wells, Mary Shelley wrote of using science to raise the dead. Perhaps Frankenstein's monster and Wells's time machine both stem from an initial period of wonder and naivete about what might be achieved using science and technology.

The various paradoxes associated with time travel make appearances throughout Gleick's narrative, but as in all of his books, Gleick has demonstrated a gift for understanding the boundaries of his arguments. He merely presents the paradoxes as philosophical artifacts, but this is where ordinary science can be used to solve the paradoxes. By performing these thought experiments, we can clarify our understanding of time.

Before "solving" the paradoxes with ordinary science, it is pertinent to define the word "paradox" itself out of existence. A paradox can only exist as a manifestation of mistaken thinking; a paradox is a tangle in the rope of logic. Straighten out the logic, and the paradox disappears; it was never a thing in itself to begin with.

The Grandfather Paradox

Can you go back in time and kill your grandfather, therefore eradicating your own existence? This is the grandfather paradox, and it can be expanded into any "change the past" plot of a science fiction story. Gleick references the philosopher Larry Dwyer, who sees a similar problem with all time travel scenarios:

> They all make the same errors, according to Dwyer. They imagine that a time traveler could change the past. That cannot happen. Dwyer can live with other difficulties created by time travel: backward causation (effects preceding their causes) and entity multiplication (time travelers and time machines crossing paths with their doubles.) But not this. "Whatever else time travel may entail," he says, "it does not involve changing the past" (p. 229).

This assumption is always based on the rather squishy premise that time travel would mess up a logical sequence of causations. The solution to the Grandfather Paradox or "entity multiplication" has more to do with the travel than the time. For all of time travel's many paradoxes, the most basic problem with the concept has been missed. A person traveling backward in time would be adding matter to the universe in a way that the Law of Conservation forbids. The matter that makes up a person existed in a different form in the past, so travelling backward in a closed system would be physically impossible.

To travel backward to an exact past, one would have to unravel one's own body to do so. A time machine would actually travel back into a past where its component parts existed before being assembled. This would add matter to that universe without actually creating any new matter. To actually travel to the past would be to return to our components, and eventually to star dust.

In other words, you did exist when your grandfather did, just not in a physical shape with a consciousness. To actually travel back to the time of your grandfather, you would need to revert to that state, and would not be capable of altering anything or killing anyone.

Calendar Problem: Future Time Travel

Science fiction hacks have been repeating the old saw that "one can travel into the future just by standing around" for years without actually contemplating what that means. No, you cannot travel into the future by just standing around because the concept of "you" is always in flux. You are moving into the future along with everyone and everything else. Consciousness may be a slippery concept, but it may be thought of as existing in terms of Julian Barbour's "nows," which consists of three-second chunks of awareness.

The question is not whether it is possible to travel into the future, but whether or not it is possible to send your current consciousness into a radically different future environment. Is it possible for a nine-year-old boy to travel 30 years into the future as a nine-year-old boy rather than arrive there as a 39 year old man? That is, could a nine-year-old be sent into to the future to meet his 39-year old self? No, as this would, again, violate the Law of Conservation. Even if the nine-year-old dies somewhere in that continuum, the "stuff" that the nine-year-old is made of will exist in some form in the future, and the molecules that he was made of cannot exist side-by-side in different formations as this would add matter to a closed system.

Multiverses (If This Is a Paradox)

What if the universe is not a closed system, but an open one that interacts with other universes in a multiverse? This question must be framed by the other time travel paradoxes. Gleick notes the work of John Hospers here:

> Time travel a la Wells is not just impossible, it is logically impossible. It is a contradiction in terms. In an argument that runs four dense pages, Hospers proves this by power of reason. "How can we be in the 20th century A.D. and the 30th century B.C. at the same time? Here already is one contradiction . . . it is not logically possible to be in one century of time and in another century of time at the same time" (p. 222).

Hospers is correct. Even though he does not invoke the Law of Conservation, he comes to the right conclusion through simple logical analysis. However, since he continues to think of human beings as singular entities, rather than as a collection of always-existing particles, he makes this mistake that Gleick simply records:

> Time is simple for Hospers. If you imagine that one day you are in the twentieth century and the next day your time machine carries you back to ancient Egypt, he retorts, "Isn't there a contradiction here again? For the next day after January 1, 1969, is January 2, 1969. The day after Tuesday is Wednesday (this analytic-'Wednesday" is defined as the day that follows Tuesday)" and so on. And he has one final argument, the last nail in time travel's logical coffin. The pyramids were built before you were born. You didn't help. You didn't even watch. "This is an unchangeable fact," says Hospers and adds, "You can't change the past. That is the crucial point: the past happened, and you can't make what happened not have happened" (p. 223).

We must think of the past in the same way that we think of our time traveler, as a compilation of particles and waves. You may not have participated in building the pyramids, but the stuff you are made of did exist at the time that the blocks got stacked, and so the physical substance that makes you up did participate, in a small way, in the making of a particular past. Again, you were always here; you just weren't you.

One proposed workaround here is the multiverse theory. Gleick highlights the work of Hugh Everett III, who developed an adolescent interest in science fiction and studied physics under John Wheeler at Princeton. Gleick sums up Wheeler's theory:

> So what if, he asks—encouraged by Wheeler, who is open as always to the weird and paradoxical—what if every measurement is actually a branching? If a quantum state can be either A or B, then neither possibility is privileged: now there are two copies of the universe, each with its own observers. The world really is a garden of forking paths. Rather than one universe, we have an ensemble of many universes. The cat is definitely alive in one universe. In another the cat is dead. "From the viewpoint of history," he writes, "all elements of a superposition (all 'branches') are 'actual,' none any more 'real' than the rest." Protective quotation marks run rampant. For Everett, the word *real* is thin ice atop a dark pond.
>
> When one is using a theory, one naturally pretends that the constructs of the theory are "real" or "exist." If the theory is highly successful (i.e. correctly predicts the sense perceptions of the user of the theory), then the confidence in the

theory is built up and its constructs tend to be identified with "elements of the real physical world." This is however a purely psychological matter.

Nonetheless, Everett had a theory and the theory made a claim: everything that can happen does happen, in one universe or another (pp. 142–143).

Everett's multiverse theory simply reifies the concept of probability. A particle can be described as it exists in one position, but since it could be in an infinite number of other positions, the current position must be compared with all other probabilistic states. This does not mean that those states actually exist at any given time. Here's the confusing part, though, and the part that unlocks a concept of time travel that obeys what we know about physics. Probabilities for the past and the future can exist in any number of nearly infinite states. As Gleick had stated earlier in the book, "Physics is made of mathematics and words, always words and mathematics. Whether the words represent 'real' entities is not always a productive question" (p. 112).

Let's remove the concept of "time travel" from its science fiction origins and rescue it from the philosophers and theoretical physicists. Let's demystify time, understand it from its historical origins, and treat time travel as a thought experiment that helps create a clearer understanding of time's role in theoretical models. Let's look at a clock and then at a ruler.

A clock is just a ruler bent into a circle; rulers measure distance, but what do clocks measure? The best answer is that clocks measure movement. Einstein's big insight was to see that an observer's experience of time, like his experience of distance, differs depending upon how fast the observer is moving. Now, if time is the measurement of movement, this would indicate that the absence of movement equals the absence of time.

What we call time is the measurement of steady movement in a universe where movement is haphazard and chaotic. Early humans used the sun and the celestial features of the night sky to keep a sense of steady movement as a way to provide perspective to the chaotic movement in the rest of the world.

Eventually this desire to keep a steady movement as a means of comparative scale led to the development of water clocks and medieval clocks, the latter of which depended upon the capture and release of energy from streams or muscles, and which over time developed greater levels of accuracy. Modern atomic clocks are calibrated to the steadiest motion we can find in the universe, which is the gradual release of electrons (otherwise known as entropy), and so are actually connected to the slow decay of the universe (which is the only certainty in physics).

In quantum calculations, the singularity "before" the Big Bang is expressed as $t = 0$. This stands for Time = 0, which means $t = 0$ Movement. This, in turn, means that t = Movement. Zero movement equals 0 time. Now, at this point, it should be interjected that movement can never be considered an absolute concept as its existence or nonexistence would be dependent upon the calibration capacity of one's measurement tool.

Having said this, we must define what we mean by "time travel." By time travel, we likely mean that a human observer could be sent, preserved in a current psychological state, into a physical reality of the past or future and to do so without causing any logical paradoxes or violating any laws of physics. Is this possible? Yes, it's possible, but not in a way that validates most science fiction scenarios.

First, we must understand that, from our perspective, where a particle or wave was three seconds ago and where it will be three seconds from now contain the same probabilities. We are never sure of the past of anything, but if a salt shaker is sitting on a table, the odds that it was on the table three seconds ago and the odds that it will be on the table three seconds from now are the same. These probabilities can change with the arrival of new factors, such as diners arriving with plates of food, but a static shaker is likely to stay where it's at.

From this, we must understand that the universe cannot be said to have a single history, but a series of probable histories that are discerned by using current evidence. As Paul Davies wrote in a 2007 article in *New Scientist* on "The Flexi-Laws of Physics":

> As Hawking has emphasized, it is a mistake to think there is a single, well-defined cosmic history connecting the big bang to the present state of the universe. . . . Rather there will be a multiplicity of possible histories, and which histories are included in the amalgam will depend on what we choose to measure today. "The histories of the universe depend on the precise question asked," Hawking said in a paper with Thomas Hertog. . . . In other words the existence of life and observers today has an effect on the past. "It leads to a profoundly different view of cosmology, and the relation between cause and effect," claims Hawking (pp. 301–303).

Think of right now as a box that connects to other boxes of past probabilities. There are infinite boxes, but only the boxes that include a history that leads to the development of life on the planet, and you as an observer, are lit up. There are several different probabilities that could have led to the universe as we observe it, but we accept only the particular pasts that led to our existence because all others would be illogical.

We can discard any past paths that did not lead to the extinction of dinosaurs, because dinosaurs are not here. There are still plenty of paths that could have led to life on the planet, and in the absence of specific evidence, some are equally probable.

Continue thinking about those boxes and this idea can be connected with Relativity Theory. Picture a line with an observer at rest represented at the bottom. His frames of particles and waves (the foundation of all the stuff around him) are divided into relatively small sections. For the purpose of simplicity, let's imagine a two-year timeline divided into 730 boxes. Now, imagine two larger boxes on top of the timeline that stretch to the same length of the 730 boxes (two big boxes on top and 730 small boxes on bottom). The two big boxes represent an observer moving at nearly light speed. The two observers move through their respective boxes and then meet at the end of the timeline.

Our faster observer only moved through two boxes of particles and waves, while our slower one moved through 730 boxes. They experienced different rates of particle and wave movements, so the observer who moved at nearly light speed only went through two boxes of movement while the slower observer experienced 730 boxes of movement. Once they both revert to the same speed, however, the faster observer would be in the future in a basically preserved psychological state.

What we are talking about here, then, is preserving an observer in a current psychological state while finding a way to move all of the particles and waves around her into either a future state or into a "past" state as defined by probabilities. This means that time travel is possible to an extent but within certain limits. First of all, to repeat, the Law of Conservation forbids a traveler from moving back to an exact past in a closed system.

However, since the laws of physics are reversible, with enough energy, it would be possible to reverse particles and waves to a previous state that is probably where they used to be, with the exception that the matter that makes up the traveler would be absent from the past state. You couldn't do this across the universe, but you could make it 1955 on Earth but 2020 on Saturn (thus answering the original question posed in this chapter).

This would not create any paradoxes because this really just puts particles into a probable past state but in future motion. This is logically sound, but physically unlikely. However, since this is a thought experiment we can imagine a traveler going "back" to 1955 (this would kill everything on the planet, by the way, and reconfigure the matter to a past state, and the odds that everything would repeat exactly the way they had before are unlikely) with a computer dictionary and a powerful battery.

She could cross check all the facts at her disposal to see if they were accurate. It would be easy to see if the right president was in office, but hard to see if every leaf on an oak tree in Iowa was where it was "supposed" to be. This would mean that the accuracy of the time travel would be determined by the only person who had seen the world in a recently past "future" state.

The one criticism this theory has received is that "time or energy" could be borrowed from the future and then used to change the past. This criticism is based upon a fundamental misunderstanding of what chemists call stochiometry, which is the balancing of chemical combinations from one form to another. For example, you can turn water, or H_2O into H, H, and O, but you cannot turn it into H, H, H, and O because that adds an element of Hydrogen that was not there originally.

The universe does not recreate itself from moment to moment with new energy and matter; it is always the same energy and matter in different configurations. The driving force of the difference from one moment to the next is the Second Law of Thermodynamics, AKA entropy, radiation, or decay. Energy and matter cannot be borrowed from either the future or the past because these are not separate states with their own energy and matter, they are separate configurations of the energy and matter that are currently here and have always been here.

"Time," defined as the measurement of movement and the notion of steady atomic movement being a rate of decay are both scientifically solid, and nothing in this thought experiment violates any known laws of physics. A teacher looking to engage students with thought experiments can use something like time travel that is intrinsically interesting, and then branch into several different fields for the purpose of developing clarity and proper analogies.

What is so interesting here is that stoichiometry, a core chemistry concept, can be applied to clear up the confusion of a time travel thought experiment. One of the reasons that time travel, and the paradox-that-wasn't involving a grandfather, typically only gets examined as a concept is through the parameters of theoretical physics. A cross-curricular approach to the thought experiment yields a new set of potential approaches to the problem. Traditional academic structures tend to discourage, or at least do not encourage, cross-curricular problem solving, but some thought experiments require such an approach if conclusions are to be reached.

With our understanding of time's appropriate roles in the theoretical models, this mental construction can now be applied to other problems and thought experiments, including infinity and the Big Bang.

KEY IDEAS AND APPLICATION TO EDUCATION

- What happens when a question, such as if "time travel" is possible, gets expanded so that the question becomes "if it is 1955 on Earth is it also 1955 on Saturn?" Answering the question expands the notion of time travel into something universal. This reveals the problem to be connected to probability theory and, as always, to the knowledge possessed by the observer.
- Time travel scenarios may be the ultimate thought experiment, because they require that theoretical physicists create a logically consistent concept of time. That consistent concept can only really be developed through a cross-curricular approach.
- As applied to the classroom, students might be invited to compare a clock and a ruler for the purpose of uncovering the historical reasons why they look so much the same.

Chapter Three

Mathematics, Infinity, and the Big Bang

Can a particle accelerate to the speed of light mathematically but not in reality? After all, according to relativity theory, a particle cannot accelerate to the speed of light. One way of thinking about this is to imagine an Olympic sprinter; in order to go faster, he will need to add muscle to his thighs, but that added muscle creates just a small amount more of drag, thus slowing the runner slightly.

Relativity theory has light as the only constant in the universe, because even if someone could travel at nearly light speed, if she turned on a flashlight, then the light beam would shoot away from her at light speed just as if she was sitting still (since we are on a moving planet). Here's the problem: Light speed is 186,000 miles per second. An object can move at 185,000.99999 miles repeating per second and alter the process of time dilation with other objects as it did so. However, the particle could never actually reach light speed. This is what physics teaches. In math, those "point 9s" become a whole number pretty quickly. First year collegiate students in the United States (and probably your average eight year old in Taiwan) know that $1/3 = 0.33333$ repeating. If you take both sides times three then you end up with $1 = 3/3 = 0.99999$. Uh oh. As the mathematician Arthur Benjamin writes:

> We say that two numbers or infinite sums are equal if they are arbitrarily close to one another. In other words, the difference between the two quantities is less than any positive number you can name, whether it be 0.01 or 0.0000001 or 1 divided by a trillion. Since the difference between 1 and 0.99999 . . . is smaller than any positive number, then mathematicians agree to call these qualities equal (p. 281).

With this logic in mind, we can see that a particle in the process of accelerating to light speed would be declared, rather quickly in fact, to have actually reached light speed. Is the problem here with physics or with mathematics?

To answer that question, we must untangle a few other knots. First of all, try to imagine calculating light speed with Roman numerals. We now use Roman numerals mainly for grandfather clocks and counting Super Bowls, but these numerals formed the basis of the entire Western mathematical system for over a thousand years. Indian mathematicians created the numbers 0–9 (the former only about 1,500 years ago), and when those numbers transferred to the Abbasid Empire (750–1258), mathematicians in the Islamic world created algebra and other forms of creative mathematical theory.

Despite the efforts of a mathematically gifted pope, Sylvester II (r. 999–1003) who tried to introduce 0–9 to Christendom, Roman numerals continued on as the major numerical system in the Christian West. Only in the early 13th century, when the Italian Fibonacci (1170–c.1250) learned Arabic mathematics and brought it north across the Mediterranean to Italy, did these new numbers become embraced by Christian bankers.

From the early 13th century until now, mathematicians and physicists have certainly used those "Arabic" numerals of 0–9 for good purposes. Mathematical systems give structure to the economy, make reasonably accurate predictions based on data, and allow for astrophysicists, engineers, and chemists to send rockets into space, extract energy from the nucleus of atoms, and keep track of the phenomena of the night sky. Such success might lead one to think, as Galileo did, that the universe is "written" in mathematics.

Yet, to believe this, we would have to think that an intellectual structure existed upon which the matter of the universe hung upon. That intellectual structure allowed for untold amounts of time to pass before a small group of former-apes managed to uncover the secrets and begin to discover previously hidden mathematical truths. Either that's the case, or mathematics is a systematic structure, like language, used to describe long-existing phenomena.

If these two things are true: 1. that 0–9 displaced Roman numerals and proved to be more useful than Roman numerals, and 2. that mathematics is an arbitrarily created structure that is descriptive and useful, then it might be true as well that our current mathematical system is as incapable of accurately understanding light speed and the potentiality to accelerate to it as Roman numerals were of picking up on the concept of compound interest.

But those decimal points in between numbers created a conundrum regarding the concept of "infinity." The word "infinity" connotes never-ending and serves a number of functions in mathematics and physics, but mostly it sucks theoretical models into a spiral of confused thinking. Infinity created a sticky muck in some of history's greatest minds. Bertrand Russell (1872–1970), for example, wrote in a 1904 response to C. J. Keyser that ". . . pure mathematics . . . [is] a mere prolongation of symbolic logic . . . there are no new axioms at all in the later parts of mathematics, including among these both ordinary arithmetic and the arithmetic of infinite numbers."

This notion, like Galileo's claim that the universe is written in numbers, creates a logical tangle. The conceptual foundation of mathematics is that certain basic concepts, derived in numbers, can then be expressed forever. When graphing, say, linear equations, an infinity symbol indicates that the line travels in a certain direction for eternity. If you understand that adding one to one equals two, then you soon come to understand that adding one to two equals three, you can then theorize that this process continues *ad infinitum*. Most people stop theorizing about the concept there.

However, the concept of infinity causes conceptual problems. The decimal points between one and two might be said to go on infinitely. How can the space between one and two and the space between zero and the number-that-never-stops-growing both be infinite? You can see the problem.

Traditionally, George Cantor gets credit for noting in 1874 that size variants exist within infinity. Some infinities are more infinite than others. Cantor gets credit for this insight, but Robert Grosseteste (1168–1253), a medieval theologian, once wrote:

> But it is possible that an infinite sum of a number be related to an infinite sum [of a number] in every number ratio and also in every non-numeric ratio. And there are infinities which are greater [plura] than other infinities, and infinities which are smaller [pacuciora] than other infinities. For the sum of all numbers both even and odd is infinite. For [the sum of the even and the odd] exceeds the sum of the even by the sum of all the odd numbers (p. 475).

A variety of thought experiments can be derived from this concept, including the Paradox of the Grand Hotel, which was conjured up in 1924 by a German mathematician named David Hilbert. Imagine a hotel with infinite rooms that is nonetheless full; two hypothetical guests show up and, while no new rooms are available, it is possible to shift guests into a new room to open one up, which is possible since there are infinite rooms, which means that rooms will be open to infinity.

This is all irrelevant, of course, because infinity, as the concept is generally defined, simply fails to exist. If someone is drawing a line on paper and runs out of ink, then the line on the paper is the extent of the infinity. One can theorize that with more ink one could draw a longer line, but if you don't have more ink then your infinity is there. The guiding analogy that clears up the confusion goes like this: "Infinity is like memory capacity."

Let's begin by defining two types of infinity. There is Theoretical Infinity, or TI, (previously known as just "infinity") and there is Real Infinity (RI). Theoretical Infinity exists only as a Platonic concept, meaning that the notion itself supposedly exists outside of actual material reality (we have to imagine something existing outside of space and time that is not made of actual matter, like atoms, for Platonic concepts to be employed).

Plato taught that all of "reality" as perceived by humans is actually an imperfect shade of a perfect world. Every object in reality has a perfect counterpart in the Realm of Forms. Every chair you sit on or coffee cup you drink out of is an imperfect copy of a perfect chair and coffee cup in the Realm.

From this, we judge the beauty and ugliness of a given object on how close its formation is to the perfect thing in the realm of forms. (Incidentally, this helps to create a pick up line that could be used on girls in a philosophy class: "You are as close to the Platonic ideal of woman as anyone I have ever seen," although, like a lot of philosophy, that line might be better in theory than in practice.)

Plato's logic is derived from mathematics, and particularly geometry. Draw a triangle on a chalkboard and everyone in the room can immediately see that A. this is a triangle, and B. this is an imperfect triangle. Where, then, is the perfect triangle that you are comparing the chalk triangle to? Plato's answer is that it must reside in the Realm of Forms. Mathematics tends to deal with perfect concepts: squares with equal sides and graphs with squares.

If you are drawing triangles on graphing paper (trigonometry), your lines aren't perfect, but the mathematical equations you derive from those lines assume perfection. Normally, this does not matter because a perfect connection between equations and reality is not necessary to make buildings stand up, stabilize bridges, or put a mechanical rover on Mars.

But when applied to the concepts of time and space, a Platonic framework generates a special kind of epistemological chaos. Plato's Realm cannot withstand logical questioning. What is the Realm of Forms made of? "Pure thought" is not an acceptable answer, as a thought actually consists of stuff like DNA, sucrose, and electricity.

If something exists, it must be made of something. These kinds of questions and assertions eventually reveal that Platonic reality is just composed of definitions. No literal perfect triangle exists in some nether realm. Rather, at some point, humans agreed upon a definition of what a triangle is and we apply that definition to shapes that we encounter. It's not much different from what happens in legal proceedings where lawyers argue whether or not an action resulting in death fits the definition of "murder" or "manslaughter" more effectively.

Like the perfect triangle, TI fails to exist. If I draw a triangle on the chalkboard, that's the only triangle that matters. There is no compelling reason to explain that chalky shape by invoking a shady shape to help in the explanation. All we ever have is RI, which is the limit of the universe's memory capacity, not TI.

For example, computers can calculate pi out to 2.7 trillion digits. That 2.7 trillionth digit is the boundary of pi's RI. If every digit of pi is a Hilbert hotel room, then shifting one guest in the first room would push someone in a (very far distant room) out. The same concept applies to prime numbers. The highest known prime number is 23,249,425 digits long. That last digit forms the RI boundary for prime numbers and, while we can conceive of the idea that another prime number might be found, the conceptual number that is the TI boundary for prime numbers does not really exist.

Here's the thing: even TI is not really "infinite" in the Platonic sense. If we stay with the prime number example, we can see that even TI must obey limits. If infinity = memory capacity, then TI ends with the memory capacity of the cognitively capable beings in the universe. If we could calculate all of the memory capacity available to humans ("we" being the only cognitively capable beings we currently know about) and all of the memory capacity in the universe (defined as "information carrying" particles in physics) and we used that capacity purely to calculate prime numbers we could theorize that another prime number could be found.

However, if this actually occurred, it would use up the collective memory capacity in the universe and would shrink the other infinities (non-prime numbers) in between the prime numbers to a single whole digit. All of the memory capacity was used up in treating them as whole numbers. One could then increase the size of those TIs in between the non-prime numbers, by moving back to 23,249,425 digits of pi, but the "infinities" would be limited to the memory capacity.

To remove the complication in this: if you only have so much ink, you can either spend it writing as many whole numbers as possible, or you can spend it writing decimal points in between whole numbers. If you increase one, then you shrink the other. The universe has a lot of ink, but the concept is the same.

Even TI is constrained by the possibility of future memory capacity. If every single wave and particle in the universe could be expressed as an information carrier, this would still create a limit to TI in the same way that it proposes a boundary to the known universe. RI's are created by whatever the real memory capacity is at the moment, but the interesting thing is that the current RI also creates a limit for TI, because we can only theorize about what would happen if we could expand our current RI to the limits of the universe's information carrying potential.

Interestingly enough, although Relativity Theory predicts that a particle trying to achieve light speed would have to become infinitely large in order to propel itself, we could actually imagine a machine of RI size, but that would mean that every particle in the universe would be used up in the propulsion, and this would leave no mass for an observer to judge whether light speed had been reached or not.

Thought experiments can only occur in the realm of thought, and Plato carved this realm originally into a cave. In the process, he shaped the shadows and false turns that have created so much confusion. One of Plato's cavernous tunnels leads all the way to a false explosion.

THE BIG BANG IS A THOUGHT EXPERIMENT

Stephen Hawking's big cosmological idea came in the form of what became known as Hawking Radiation. Hawking found that black holes emit tiny particles, which is another way of saying that Black Holes radiate, which is another way of saying that even Black Holes are subject to the Second Law of Thermodynamics (everything trends toward entropy). To call Hawking the inheritor of Newton and Einstein, as journalists often do, is to misunderstand the concept of scientific achievement.

Newton developed a theory of physics that explained planetary motion; Einstein created two types of Relativity Theory and untangled the paradox of the photoelectric effect; Hawking pointed out that Black Holes are subject to the Second Law of Thermodynamics. We already knew this because everything is subject to the Second Law of Thermodynamics, and his pointing this out is about as significant as someone saying that gravity also applies to toasters.

However, Hawking Radiation leads to an interesting thought experiment because black holes are the closest analogy we have to the early universe; because time is the measurement of movement, and because gravity affects movement, how do we think about the early universe with black holes as a guiding analogy?

One commonly reads, especially in so-called "Big History" publications, that a Big Bang occurred 13.8 billion years ago. The phrase "Big Bang" was created sarcastically by the English astronomer Fred Hoyle (1915–2001) in a

1949 British radio interview. The concept was derived from Edwin Hubble's (1889–1953) finding that red-shifted light that was omitted from the edges of the universe, and this indicated that the universe expands. If everything in the universe expands, then everything must have once been closer together. Extrapolate that logic to a singularity and we get a particle of RI density.

Traditional Big Bang cosmology explains the Big Bang as occurring with an explosion. Hoyle believed in a "steady state" universe where the laws of physics remained largely even and unchanging. The concept of an expanding universe causes epistemological problems that physicists and astronomers, even now, have never really come to terms with. Here's the first problem posed by the concept of an expanding universe: it means that gravity used to be stronger.

Again, no fancy thinking is required to make this deduction. Newton's famous Inverse Square Law Equation posits that with G, or gravity, as a constant, the further that an object moves from the center of gravity, the less effect that gravitational pull has on that object. Rockets that shoot away from Earth require enormous thrust to escape the initial pull of gravity, but much less as the rocket gets further away. If the universe is expanding, then objects with gravitational pull constantly pull away from each other, and thus, gravity continually gets weaker. If gravity is getting weaker, then that must mean it was once stronger.

Consider another time travel scenario. A group of scientists send a time traveler back to the Age of the Dinosaurs, and the traveler comes back as canned spam in a time machine that's been crushed by the increasing force of gravity, or else the traveler dies of "the bends" in the same way that a deep sea diver who surfaces too quickly would. Does this sound absurd?

Well, we know that if we sent a time traveler back to a singularity point before the so-called "Big Bang," she would be crushed by gravity. At some point in that continuum we must reach a point where someone who currently lives would go back to a crush point; how far back would that be?

The interesting thing about gravity is that it acts on all things at once, including time keeping instruments, and so no one in the current era can possibly notice the effect of the gravitational change. Again, any instrument of measurement would be subject to gravitational pull. We can't put a clock or an observer outside of the universe for a point of reference. That being said,our cells must evolve and adapt to a changing level of gravity in the same way that the cells of sharks or homing pigeons have evolved to be in sync with the earth's magnetic field.

Consider this point: in physics, the most basic equation is Speed = Distance/Time. If you are going 55 miles an hour, that's your speed. But "time" differs radically depending upon gravitational forces. A clock ticks differently on the edge of a black hole than it does on Earth and this ruins the point of comparison. Now, with black holes, we can understand that our Earthling conception of time is different, but the problem is that time is to human observers doesn't change because we are inside the concept. From our current standpoint, time in the "earliest" moments of the universe would be different from now, which means that we cannot extrapolate Speed = Distance/Time either into the past or the future because the rate of gravitational force shifts. If we do, we might end up thinking that a slow process looks like an explosion.

It's hard to think about, but our mathematics is only a few centuries old and it describes the conditions that have existed for the last few centuries. We know that the universe is decaying over time, that gravity is losing to entropy, but we do not know how to adjust our calculations to that reality because our mathematics is created from a historical vantage point.

This is kind of like if geographers in the mid-eighteenth century tried to solve certain historical puzzles without factoring in continental drift (because they did not know). It's hard to imagine that tectonic plates shift the continents away from each other at a half inch or so a year, and hard to understand that cartography gave us a picture of a particular period, but without that understanding nothing makes sense. Hold this thought experiment in a pattern of neurons for a moment, because we will come back to it soon.

To return to an earlier point, what we call time is a steady reference point for movement in a world where movement is chaotic and herky-jerky. Let's call "time as a reference point" theoretical time and "real time" temperature. The First Law of Thermodynamics is "Work creates heat." The measurement of actual movement in an object is its temperature, but since that movement is localized, we measure it against theoretical movement in the form of time.

It is not possible to place a theoretical reference point outside of the universe, we should not consider theoretical time at all in physics, but rather temperature as it would have occurred in the realm of overwhelming gravity.

Here's where it gets weird. From the vantage point of a particle in the early universe, it might have "looked like" an explosion, but from the vantage point of current scientists, it actually looks like an impossibly slow drip. We are, theoretically, outside of the gravitational conditions of the early universe and therefore in a kind of Platonic realm, but we are developing mathematical equations that simply fail to fit those early conditions because we are trying to understand the scale through theoretical time. Here's what this means with a little bit of historical background:

Edwin Hubble discovered two things of significance: A. galaxies exist outside of our own Milky Way, and B. those galaxies move away from Earth. This means that either the Earth is at the center of the universe, the epicenter of a cosmic blast, or that everything is expanding away from each other at once like the images on the outside of a balloon would be. The balloon analogy is often invoked, most famously in Hawking's books, but it is misleading because it posits an internal force pushing out the universe as is the case with an explosion, but this is not what happens.

Instead of blowing up from the inside the universe radiates at the edges. We need to understand the overwhelming power of entropy by reviewing the contribution of Arthur Eddington (1882–1944). Eddington posited that the direction of time can only be discerned, from a universe-eye-view, by the expansion of entropy. Take any cross-section of the universe that you want and frame it; hour by hour the one constant is that every particle in that cross-section tends toward entropy. Several points can be made from this insight:

A. The Periodic Table can be viewed by an element's resistance to entropy. So-called stable elements omit radiation slowly while unstable elements radiate quickly. Entropy acts on every element, but at different rates. The rate of entropy can be discerned through the temperature of specific elements compared to each other for the purpose of creating a frame of reference. Hence, the use of atomic clocks to keep a constant sense of motion/time.

B. What we call "energy" is really the capture of another object's decay through entropy. Entropy acts upon the sun and the force of its radiation is captured by biological material on Earth and treated, temporarily, as energy. (This is a point always overlooked by religionists; it's rather inconvenient to have decay as the core force of the universe. In the beginning there was entropy, not light.) The human body, for example, is in such a constant state of decay that entropy from the natural world must constantly be captured in the form of calories and turned into cellular reconstruction. Entropy will win over all of us.

C. The human mind must be evolutionarily connected somehow to the force of entropy, otherwise we would not sense a forward motion of time. We have only a three second window of consciousness where we can process thoughts, and the images in our minds that are assumed to be memories very well could be something else. How do we know that we can remember the past but not see the future? What if we can see the future but not remember anything, and your current age represents how many years you have until you crawl backward into your mother's womb and dissolve into nothing? You don't know this, but our concept of forward time must be connected to the continued force of entropy in the universe somehow.

Muller writes:

> The Second Law [of Thermodynamics] states that there is a quantity called entropy that, for a collection of objects, either stays constant with time or increases. Contrast that with energy, which always remains constant. Energy can shift from one thing to another, but the sum of the energy of all the objects doesn't change. Unlike the First Law, the Second Law is not absolute, but only probabilistic. Although it can be violated, the likelihood of a violation for large-scale collections of particles is negligibly small.
>
> Entropy and time increase together. They are correlated. That was known. Eddington's new speculation was that entropy was responsible for the arrow of the time, the fact that time moves forward rather than backward. He argued that the Second Law of Thermodynamics explains why we remember the past rather than the future (p. 98).

In this passage, there seems to be some confusion regarding entropy and energy, which are not separate forces at all. Energy is entropy that is temporarily captured to create a pocket of structural order. Gravity might be thought of as the opposite of entropy, since, like a strong nuclear force, it works to temporarily prevent entropy. Gravity cannot cease to exist, only change form, which poses the question: what happens to gravity as entropy extends? It doesn't cease to exist, but merely stretches itself thinner and thinner.

Now we must apply all of these concepts to the singularity that existed before time and the Big Bang. If a Black Hole is closely analogous to that singularity event, then we should bring our entire conception of the universe into this conceptual framework. In 1974, Hawking predicted that black holes radiate. This process can be described in different ways, most popularly as a particle and an anti-particle being split apart at the event horizon of a black hole.

However, it's easiest, as the physicist Jacob Bekenstein pointed out, to simply think of a black hole as shrinking due to entropy. Black holes radiate and as they do, they shrink. The slowness of this process cannot be described in human concepts of speed. Now, from the perspective of the event horizon, the leaking of Hawking radiation, no matter how slight, can be also seen as propulsion.

As particles escape, they carry with them a small amount of gravitational force. The farther the particle gets from the core of the gravity pulling on it, the faster it will move. Over time, the edges of a universe created by entropy will begin to speed up and expand.

The farther that particles get from their gravitational source, the faster they will move. And since those particles contain mass, they also pull with a certain force of gravitation. Subsequent pockets of Hawking radiation will not just be propelled by entropy but also dragged by the gravity of the mass that just escaped. This model produces an expanding universe without any false conceptions of Platonic time.

If the Universe began with a slow drip of Hawking radiation, rather than a Big Bang, then it eventually developed conditions that allowed for humans to evolve, and that's about all that we can say for certain. Speaking of lack of certainty, we can use the same philosophical foundations that informed our study of the universe's origins to understand one of the most complex components of theoretical physics: the notorious double-slit experiment. (Warning to readers: this section will involve some hypothetical dead cats.)

The double-slit experiment is not a thought experiment; it's a real experiment that has been performed over two centuries. Physicists express mild befuddlement over the experiment, which is not a big deal because being mildly befuddled is part of the job description for physicists, but New Age (rhymes with "sewage") philosophers almost always invoke the double slit experiment as proof that the human minds possesses some sort of agency over the universe.

The double-slit experiment involves shining light, or firing electrons, through two slits and then observing the pattern created on a sensitive screen. On one level, physicists find this interesting because light, for example, acts as a wave going through the slits and the wavelengths of the beam cancel each other out, but light hits the screen like a particle. This "wave-particle" duality caused a problem for physicists who wanted to trap light in either a cognitive jar labeled "wave" or another jar labeled "particle." This is not a problem for light, but a problem for physicists: light acts like neither a particle nor a wave; light acts like light.

The reason that newage philosophers find the double-slit experiment to be so sexy is because light, or electrons, or protons, or whatever, exist in wave- like form until measured, when they then solidify their position into a particle form. That's what makes the newagers jump up and down, pointing and shouting, "Look! These particles know you are looking at them! Your mind affects the universe!" (Occasionally an amateur theologian will read a book of physics and then grandly declare that the universe must need an observer who sits outside of it, a god of some sort, in order to break down the probability fields into a single existence.)

This strange behavior of light and other small particles (a word we'll use for convenience) led to one of the strangest and most famous of thought experiments: that of Schrodinger's Cat. This thought experiment, first derived by the Austrian physicist Erwin Schrödinger in 1935, has been around so long that theorists speak and write of it in almost solemn tones.

This reverence may take away from some of the outright weirdness: if you began with just the concept behind Schrödinger's thought experiment, you could probably think of several dozen ways to explain it without ever invoking a cat or poison, which makes me wonder just what was up with Schrödinger in the first place. It's sort of like explaining long division by saying, "Let's imagine that you drop twenty horses out of an airplane and fifteen of those horses hit the ground and explode, but five fall into a lake and swim to shore.

That would mean that fifteen of the twenty left their guts all over the ground. Of the twenty, five survived, which means that fifteen goes into twenty only one time with a remainder of five." One might even think that the concept of division could be better explained using pizza slices instead of dead horses.

Nonetheless, the thought experiment is set up thusly: a cat, a vial of poison, a radioactivity detector (i.e., a Geiger counter), and some kind of radioactive material are put into a box. If the detector senses radiation, then the vial of poison breaks and the cat dies. If not, the cat lives.

This morbid thought experiment was developed as a way of thinking about probabilities. To an observer outside of the box, the cat exists temporarily in a state of both being alive and dead. Only when the box is opened, and the observer can see whether the kitty made it or not, do the probabilities break down into a single history. One can use different examples to explain the same concept.

A person who wants to watch a boxing match, but can't stay up late enough to see it, might record the fight and watch it the next morning. If Boxer A is a 3 to 1 favorite to defeat Boxer B, then the next morning the odds are still 3 to 1 for the person who has not yet seen the fight. Those odds are the same to that person because even though the outcome has been decided, it is not known to that person.

In terms of light photons or electrons, they exist in probability fields that predict their states. In 1927, Werner Heisenberg (a German, as just about everyone in 20th century physics was) developed his Uncertainty Principle. Heisenberg stated that we can either know where a particle is or we can know how fast it's going, but not both. Either speed or position will always be either unknown. This causes confusion when applied to the double slit experiment, because Heisenberg's Uncertainty Principle contains a slight misstatement.

We can never know where a particle *is*, only where it *was*. When a particle hits a detector and breaks from a wave probability (from the perspective of the observer) into an actual position (where it acts like a particle), the information must travel through the detector into the eyes of an observer and then be processed into information that is comprehended by the human mind. It takes about three seconds for that to happen; three seconds is not much in the macro-world, but when dealing with particles that travel near light speed, a photon could be nearly half a billion miles away by the time a human scientist made sense of where it just was.

We are always looking at the past, never the present, because of a process lag. This doesn't matter in the "real" macro-world that we live in, because things like bananas and car keys don't zip across the universe, but at the micro-level this lag obviously does matter.

Since the universe consists of particles and waves in the aggregate, what is true for micro-particles is true for everything. We never understand the universe where it is, only where it was. This misleads us into thinking that we are looking at a universe with an absolute position. Only when we think about the universe beyond the human-understanding-time-lag, do we see that particle exist in probability fields. We aren't forcing photons to pick a slit, or a position, only recognizing where they were recently.

When we speak of an object, such as a car for example, we speak of it as a concrete thing rather than as something in a state of flux. We fail to recognize that, over time, the car changes in incremental ways. If I go into a diner and leave my car in the parking lot, I expect to find the car in the lot when I finish eating.

The fact that microparticles somewhere in the car might have zipped across the universe, or that a random neutrino might have smacked an electron out of a molecule somewhere in the steering wheel, never occurs to me because such actions would not affect my perception or use of the car. In the aggregate, the car is stable, even if the individual car particles are not.

We speak of people the same way, even though we know that men completely update their cells every five years; we don't say "I remember Version 6.0 of Dave; he was more fun than Version 8.0." We speak of ourselves as if there is a level of continuity that doesn't exist.

For the sake of understanding probabilities, let's return to the hypothetical car. The odds that any random particle of the car could be affected by a neutrino are pretty small, but not zero. The odds that any two particles would be affected are longer, and the more factors we add, the longer the odds get. So the odds that I would go into a diner and return with my car reduced to metal pudding as a result of neutrino bombardment would be extremely bad (to a degree where the odds are probably X to 1, where X would exceed the number of known particles in the universe).

Those aggregate odds give us a sense of permanency that does not equip the human mind to think about micro-particles. Nothing mysterious is happening, with the double slit experiment or anything else in science. As always, we just need to adjust our minds to the circumstances.

Too often in the study of science, students are not necessarily encouraged to study the metacognitive aspects of the study of light, for example, and instead find themselves immersed only in the mathematics of propulsion or the mathematics inherent in studying wavelengths.

Mathematics only seems to be mechanical when one is answering equations on a piece of paper. If one picks the paper up and looks behind it, then one can see the epistemological questions that make mathematics so fascinating. A math teacher who explains the arrows on a Cartesian graph in terms of infinity could begin with the deep philosophy of the concept. Ultimately, mathematics is subject to the same errors of analogical logic that can cause confusion in other subject areas, and a false analogy regarding infinity is one of the most serious.

Thought experiments are fairly well known in the sciences, but continually underutilized in politics and issues involving identity. Let's turn our attention away from theoretical physics and develop the force of thought experiments to be utilized in politics and identity politics.

KEY POINTS AND APPLICATION TO EDUCATION

- "Infinity" really is a thought experiment, one that's based upon Platonic principles that have confused the mathematics and theory. The confusion can be cleared up by creating a new analogy where "infinity is like memory capacity," and from this we can posit a "real infinity" and a "theoretical infinity." This helps to explain how infinity can have different sizes.
- The Big Bang is a thought experiment. Although it is often mistaken for an actual event, the Big Bang is a probabilistic event based on current evidence. When the concept of time is understood to be a "measure of movement" as has been previously posited, then the theoretical problems associated with a "bang" dissipate.
- From an epistemological standpoint, the famous "double slit" experiment really is not as mysterious as NewAge "philosophers" try to make it out to be. The processing speed of the human mind lags behind the movement of particles and waves by about three seconds, which is a very long time in

the quantum world. We are always seeing particles where they were, not where they are, and that is what accounts for the observer effect on quanta of light.

- For students, these are good lessons in metacognition. How do students know what they know? The only way to uncover a metacognitive perspective is through the study of history, and that ultimately unites disciplines.

Chapter Four

Politics

Imagine a political candidate for the House of Representatives with no position at all on any issues. This political candidate will not run with any major political party. Her one pledge is, after her election, that she will post one question on her secure website, and her constituents can answer.

"How often do you want me to vote with the Republicans?" The aggregate numbers will give her a percentage between, as the voters will be asked, "0% and 100% of the time," and she will apply that percentage to the average number of issue votes that occur over a typical two-year term and put that into a random generator. So, if her constituents want her to vote with the Republicans 72% of the time, by the end of her tenure in office the random vote-generator should be able to hit that number just about exactly.

When she is up for reelection, her constituents will have no reason to toss her out if they don't like her votes. They can simply re-elect her and then change the percentage of the time they want her to vote with the Republicans. The Congresswoman will vote with the random algorithm every time, no matter how important the legislation or how personally opposed she might be to whatever new law comes before the House.

Meanwhile, she would be free to roam through her House district, talking with people about their needs and then crafting legislation to meet those needs. It could be the case, of course, that she would end up voting against laws that she herself had proposed, but that is okay because, despite its minor faults, this approach to politics is far superior to the current party-based system.

In order to explain why this political thought experiment should be turned into reality, and how it will untangle the problems and paradoxes in modern American federal law and politics, we need to go back and discuss the development of the American Constitution as it was originally conceived in thought experiments. The best way to do this is through a structured sequence of logical connections. The Declaration of Independence declares:

We hold these truths to be self-evident, that all men are created equal, that they are endowed by their Creator with certain unalienable Rights, that among these are life, Liberty, and the pursuit of happiness.- That to secure these rights, Governments are instituted among Men, deriving their just powers from the consent of the governed.

These certainly rank as the most misread lines in all of world history; especially the "all men are created equal . . ." part, which Jefferson and the Founders almost certainly construed in a radically different way from modern readers. Historical documents cannot be read outside of their context; to do so amounts to a kind of documental illiteracy that is similar to trying to understand biological processes without the framework of evolutionary theory.

Historians harp on this a lot, but broad historical learning and understanding must be developed in a scholar before documents can actually be understood for their original meanings. If ". . . all men are created equal . . ." functions as the point of a logical spear, it must be understood that a long shaft of historical wood is behind it.

The butt-end of that spear begins with the Roman Emperor Constantine (272–337), who considered the traditional Roman polytheism to be a contributor to the dysfunction and disunion of the empire as it existed in the fourth century. After defeating (and beheading the corpse of) his brother-in-law, Constantine eventually elevated himself to be sole emperor of the Roman Empire and elevated Christianity to the official religion of Rome. From the time of the Edict of Milan (313) to the Protestant Reformation in 1517, Christianity formed the core Western civilization.

The catholic Church (the small "c" denotes an adjective, as in "universal") formed in the image of the Roman Empire, with the Bishophood of Rome eventually evolving into the papacy. In the fifth century, as the state devolved (heading toward an eventual governmental collapse in the year 476) into feudal (the root of that word, with a wink, is "feud") estates. These provincial states formed from the various Germanic and Viking clans that tore off sections of the Roman Empire's corpse and growled and snapped at each other while gnawing its bones. In this environment, the office of the papacy, regardless of the occupant, evolved into a political force.

Constantine, like most rulers, cannot be described as intellectually curious. He probably only knew two things about Christianity: 1. a good many of his soldiers professed the Christian faith, and 2. Christianity featured a single god, and this meshed well with Constantine's plan to pass off the notion of "one god, one emperor" to the Roman people. Christianity, however, posed a problem as a political force, in that it existed, even if in a watery way, for about three centuries before Constantine took power.

Although Christians possessed no Bible, no single narrative of the life and teachings of Jesus (there are about 24 gospels that we know of, even if only four made it into the Bible), and no clear central theocracy at the time of Constantine, their beliefs did possess a core message of sorts that may be summed up like this: "Good behavior will not be rewarded in this life, but it will be in the next life."

The biblical Jesus ranks as a literary, rather than historical, character (just like Yahweh, Abraham, Moses, etc.), but the message that comes across in his literature cannot be conceived of as a guidebook for how to gain and exercise political power. In exactly none of the fictional tales known as the gospels does Jesus rise to the position of a Roman governor; the political authorities execute him. The Sermon on the Mount praises the poor and hungry and promises the Earth, eventually (any day now), to the meek.

By trying to co-opt the Christian narrative into the power structure of the Roman elite, Constantine created conditions in which any emperor could be accused of hypocrisy by the people and be held to a moral standard as defined by the Church. Constantine, without knowing it, created conditions by which a "Christian" emperor could be held accountable by the institution that declared itself capable of defining what "Christian" meant.

Just a few decades after the Christianization of Rome and the death of Constantine, in the year 390, Western civilization faced a defining moment. Germanic refugees from the northeast, searching for territory after being driven out by the Huns, threatened Rome's stability by settling in the Empire's territory. In an attempt to assimilate these peoples, Theodosius conscripted them into the military. In the year 390, when the people of Thessalonica revolted over an incident involving the arrest of a popular chariot racer, Theodosius did what emperors always did: he ordered, from his residence in Milan, his troops to massacre the rebels.

After issuing the order, either Constantine's conscience or his better sense caught up with him and he attempted to rescind his words. Unfortunately, his second order traveled too late to stop the blades of his soldiers. The Goths, foreigners, chopped up several thousand Romans in Thessalonica. For most of history, such an action would have induced a shrug, maybe even a yawn in the elite power structure; what else could be done when the masses got out of hand? Except now, in Christian Rome, a confrontation of singular importance occurred.

In 390, the papacy existed only embryonically. However, Ambrose claimed the title of Bishop of Milan which gave him spiritual and bureaucratic authority over large sections of a newly formed Christian church that possessed institutional strength. Ambrose is now considered a saint and one of the great fathers of the Catholic Church; he seems to have been sincere in his revulsion over the massacre perpetrated by Theodosius. Ambrose took a stance by refusing to perform Mass with Theodosius present, and then took up his pen and wrote a letter to the emperor explaining why.

Then, when Theodosius tried to enter a Milanese Church, Ambrose confronted the emperor about the massacre and refused to let Theodosius cross the threshold of the Church, in either a physical or spiritual capacity, until the emperor asked forgiveness and performed acts of penance.

Eventually Theodosius, either through a genuine belief that he had sinned (this might have been the case, given that he did originally take back the order on his own accord, even if it was too late) or through a fear of what a church-led vote of "no-confidence" in his regime would entail, did beg forgiveness and issued a law that indicated that thirty days must pass between the assigning of a declaration of death, and the actual execution of any citizens of Rome.

This confrontation, depicted in two famous early 17th century paintings by Rubens and Van Dyck, remains underappreciated as a shaper of Western civilization. By forcing Theodosius to submit to the will of the Church, Ambrose established a sort of balance of power that would, along with other factors, make western civilization unique in the sense that political institutions of the West harbored an ideology that rivaled the political figures rather than upholding them. Contrast this with China, where the Han Emperor Wu Di (156–87 BCE) established Confucianism as the core ideology of the Chinese court.

Like Constantine, Wu Di co-opted an already-existing ideology in the service of political power. Unlike Constantine, Wu Di chose an ideology that fit with the actual process of governing in the real world, with real political power. Confucius (551–479 BCE) taught a masculine philosophy about hierarchy, order, and power. Confucius wrote nothing about an afterlife, and judged actions to be right or wrong not based upon theological concerns, but rather on the basis of whether or not the actions created social stability. Confucianism, in short, states that: A. the father should lead the household, B. the emperor should lead China, and C. China should lead the rest of the world.

In practice, this meant that Chinese emperors would never have to face down any Confucian version of the Bishop of Milan. While Wu Di established the famous Chinese system for civil service exams, this produced bureaucrats who were then absorbed into China's political structure; they went inside the Han Dynasty's machinery of power rather than, as was the case in Christendom, into a separate apparatus entirely.

Confucian bureaucrats could and often did manipulate weak-minded emperors and they did maneuver politically, but no full-scale institution developed that rivaled the power of the emperor or questioned the validity of the emperor's power to rule. In Christendom, eventually both the monarchs and the popes would claim that their power to rule came directly from God. In China, only the emperor's power came from Heaven; the Confucian scholars could only advise the ruler on how to exercise his power, they could not check his power by exercising authority in their own right.

Likewise, Islam, if we ignore the historically-unsubstantiated "Islamic traditions" written down only centuries later by Arabs who found themselves in political control of North Africa and Central Asia, was wholly invented by an 8th and 9th century ruling class that needed a foundational myth, and a mythical founder, to provide an origin story. Only in the Christian West did the power structure adapt an already-existing ideology, one incompatible with the exercise of actual power, at the center of society.

Meek peacemakers never fared well in medieval times, and the incompatibility of Christian doctrine with the exercise of political power led to the hypocrisy. In 1517, Luther broke the foundations of Christendom, and for the next 160 years, Western civilization possessed no core.

Violence and creativity, the latter often taking the form of military advancements in both technology and tactics, marked that time period. Given that about 90% of the natives in America died of Eurasian diseases and that the Thirty Years War (1618–1648) of Germany may have been the deadliest, in terms of the percentage of the population that died, in all of world history, the era might be described as apocalyptic.

Protestantism, more than anything, redefined Western civilization during those years. Protestants who could not bring themselves to believe that the pope received his power from God could not get themselves to believe that the king did either. Protestants selected their leaders from the congregation and in England, where barons and parliamentarians never put much truck in the old divinely-inspired ruler trick, this mattered more than anywhere else.

Not only did the parliamentarians hack off the head of King Charles I one cold day in January of 1649, they got all uppity about parliamentary control not long afterward. The English Civil Wars and the subsequent period of civil strife defy any neat timeline. The English people, who were by then almost rabid coffee drinkers and voracious readers, proved to be better informed than the barefoot huckleberries the Middle Ages.

For that was the other gift of the Reformation: Luther and his successors believed that in order to cut out the Catholic bureaucracy, all those theologians and mass-peddlers, one needed to be able to read the Bible for oneself. This meant, for the first time, that large-scale education became a priority for a well-defined group of people.

After over a century and a half of strife where nothing seemed to be holding society up, two new pillars, those of science and democracy, formed at the same place in the same time. In 1687, Newton published his *Principia Mathematica*, thus proving (even if this cannot be described as his intent) that science and natural philosophy possessed descriptive powers far beyond those of theology (none of the holy books or ancient sages knew about the landmass directly across the Atlantic, and this rather harmed their veracity; sages never like experiments), and in 1688, England's Glorious Revolution created parliamentary rule.

That Glorious Revolution, by the way, lacked the majesty that its name implies. After the beheading of Charles I in 1649, the Puritans, led by Oliver Cromwell, outlawed fun entirely, and when Cromwell died (1658), the rather befuddled English simply invited the son of Charles I, the spectacularly named Charles II, to be come in and take things over as long he promised not to do much.

When Charles-the-sequel died, heirless (and not for lack of trying), his brother James II became king. Problematically Catholic and catastrophically stupid, James II finally provoked the English parliament into inviting the Protestant sovereign of the Netherlands, William, and his lovely wife Mary to invade England and drive off James II. James had a tendency to attract humiliation, and the fact that Mary was his daughter was only one of his problems, the other two being that he lacked both a brain and a spine (an almost hereditary problem with the Tudors).

When James II escaped to France, where his Catholicism allowed him toleration, the English parliament corralled most of the nascent empire's political power into the House of Commons and then shut the door behind it. The sovereign(s) could live in luxury but needed to be quiet about it and this, more or less, can be called the beginning of modern democratic institutions. A year later, in 1689, an English Bill of Rights went into legal effect and the world had a new example of how a government might work.

The purpose of stating this is to point out that the Enlightenment, as a philosophical and social movement, affected Parliament's thinking not at all. John Locke wrote his treatise on the social contract only after the Glorious Revolution and he, *post facto*, turned a treasonous parliamentary power grab into a justified revolution. Social contract theory became the new central thesis in 17th and 18th century political theory, and it was from this secondary (to Protestantism) philosophy that the revolutionaries in America and France, in 1776 and 1789 respectively, drew as justification for their rebellions. Two points come from this historical context:

1. The Enlightenment philosophers cannot be described as human-rights advocates; they simply described societal interactions and the interaction between the "people" (however narrowly defined) in terms of a contract law. In this era's writing, discussions about human rights remained limited to philosophizing about the natural state of humanity.

Darwin failed to exist at the time, as did anthropology, but the discovery of new continents in the form of North America, South America, and Australia that were full of people who lived largely without cities and, therefore, civilization, brought up questions about what the natural state of humanity had been before the advent of states. This would, eventually, have deep implications since both the Catholic Church and the various Protestants believed human nature to be evil; they argued only about what, either "good works" as defined by the Catholic Church, or "faith alone" as defined by Luther, could wash away humanity's sinful nature. However, a detailed analysis of what the Enlightenment philosophers wrote about human nature would be an unwelcome deterrent in this chapter; it's enough to say that they were not proclaiming universal equality among humans.

2. The American colonists liked English parliamentary monarchy. The American Revolution did not begin as a rejection of Great Britain, or of a monarchy, but instead formed out of the colonial frustration at not being able to join a governmental system they admired. The phrase, "no taxation without representation," popular in both the Ireland and the American colonies, reflected a desire to be involved in Great Britain's representative democracy. It was the frustration of that desire that led to the American Revolution. This brings us to Thomas Jefferson's scandalously misread sentence in the Declaration of Independence.

Some politically minded Christians, having scoured the Constitution and found neither the word God nor the word of God, have settled on the reference to a "Creator" that appears in the Declaration of Independence as a wedge to drive home their larger point that the United States is a Christian nation. Liberals, ever concerned with equality, like the phrase "all men are created equal. . . ." Neither side is likely deliberate in their misinterpretations, but if a shallow understanding of something suits your purposes, then why study more deeply?

Jefferson's sentiment, "We hold these truths to be self-evident, that all men are created equal, that they are endowed by their Creator with certain unalienable rights . . ." was not intended as a grand statement about human rights but rather as a logical syllogism. The Declaration is like a page from one of Leonardo Da Vinci's notebooks that must be held up to a mirror to be read. The mirror to the Declaration is the doctrine of the divine right of kings. Once the Declaration is held up to its reflection, the real purpose of the document becomes apparent—and the place that formal logical thinking, rather than a belief in a vague divinity, has in American history can be restored to its proper status.

The simple concept of the divine right of kings likely began right along with the inception of human civilization. It's the assertion that the ruler derives his or her right to govern from supernatural authority. One person, the ruler, is elevated above everyone else and this is justified by saying that the deity-of-choice from the people decreed this. This leads to the following syllogism: A. the monarch gets his/her powers to rule from God. B. Therefore, anything that the monarch says or does is sanctioned by God, and C. therefore people should be subjected to the power of the monarch and serve and obey him or her.

In contrast, here are the first two paragraph of the Declaration of Independence:

> We hold these truths to be self-evident, that all mean are created equal, that they are endowed by their Creator with certain unalienable Rights, that among these are Life, Liberty, and the pursuit of Happiness. That to secure these rights, Governments are instituted among Men, deriving their just powers from the Consent of the governed.
>
> That whenever any Form of Government becomes destructive of these ends, it is the Right of the People to alter or to abolish it, and to institute a new Government, laying its foundation on such principles and organizing its powers un such form, as to them shall seem most likely to effect their safety and Happiness.

If the divine right syllogism can be thought of as a building, then its foundation would be the premise that the king (of Britain, in this case) obtained his powers to rule from God. Let us pause a moment and remember this:

The Declaration of Independence was written to King George III.

This must be set off by itself because, without an understanding of who the intended audience is, no historians can study the meaning of any document. The five-word phrase "all men are created equal" was written specifically to a man who derived his, however meager, powers from a political philosophy that stated he was unequal. How would King George III have read that phrase—as a general philosophical statement about the nature of humanity, or as a direct attack on his notion of divinely sanctioned privilege?

Jefferson, a slaveholder, is often called a hypocrite for having written lines about universal equality. Jefferson the slaveholder cannot be defended, but Jefferson the logician should be. When he wrote the Declaration, his intent was probably not to make a grand humanistic pronouncement. Instead, he was likely creating the base for a syllogism.

Again, a king was the primary audience for the Declaration, and the Continental Congress was telling the king that no man could be born above others. That is, the rebels in the Colonies no longer accepted the philosophical base of the king's authority. The Declaration is the divine right inversed. Jefferson's syllogistic god gave power not to one person but to all persons. It created a new base for a political syllogism, one that looks like this: (1) All men are given rights by God.

Given this new base, if all men have rights granted by a creator, then what is the purpose of government? If government is not sanctioned by a higher power, then it cannot grant rights to people. So, what is its function? Obviously, it must be to protect natural rights. So now have the second part of the syllogism: (2) Therefore, governments exist to protect those rights. And finally, the logical conclusion of this syllogism, but one which is rarely spelled out, is: (3) Therefore, citizens are under no obligation to obey governments that violate their "God-given" rights and in fact are justified in overthrowing those governments.

The reference to a creator here is intended as syllogism-based, something that someone as schooled in logic and rhetoric as Jefferson (and Adams and Franklin for that matter) would have readily understood as a necessary precondition for a logical argument. Hence, it should not be taken to refer specifically to a deity. Nor should it be inferred that one must believe in a rights-giving god in order to believe that humans have the right to "life, liberty, and the pursuit of happiness."

One can obviously believe in the sanctity of human liberties without believing that they were handed down by a divinity. After all, it was disbelief in a tyrant-sanctioning god that was the real rub between the American continentals and the Europeans. Or one can just as easily posit, as many do, that such a god is directly in opposition to human rights.

This Declaration-as-syllogism interpretation is not new, but has a proud history. America's finest president, Abraham Lincoln, seemed to base his entire American philosophy around this vision of the Declaration. Consider what he said in one of his debates against Stephen Douglas:

> That is the issue that will continue in this country when these poor tongues of Judge Douglas and myself shall be silent. It is the eternal struggle between these two principles—right and wrong—throughout the world . . . from the beginning of time. . . . The one is the common right of humanity and the other the divine right of kings. . . . No matter in what shape it comes, whether from a king who seeks to bestride the people of his own nation and live by the fruit of their labor, or from one race of men as an apology for enslaving another race, it is the same tyrannical principle.

Lincoln's words remind us that the sentiments in the Declaration's syllogism run counter to any form of tyrannical logic, whether it comes from the government, religions, or coercive owners of labor. The American principle is more revolutionary and more antagonistic toward authority of any kind than is commonly understood today. Far from being a religiously inspired document, the Declaration of Independence is a stunning example of how, at our country's birth, rigorous, logical, and ethical reasoning were applied to derive concepts of justice.

Our Constitution and our evidence-based system of law are both built upon the core philosophy so succinctly stated in the Declaration. God cannot be found in the Constitution, but careful reasoning can be, and thank logic for that.

With the philosophy of the Declaration established, a war still had to be won, and then a Constitution created. The Constitution as originally written, contained two major flaws. The first, well-known, is that the Constitution allowed for slavery. James Madison's original draft of the Constitution contained no guarantees for basic liberties. It didn't need one, because the onus should be on the government, he surmised, to provide a justification for taking away rights, and an informed electorate should not tolerate this.

Only when James Mason and the anti-Federalists started harping about an unnecessary bill of rights did Madison sit down to create one. Those original ten amendments, so often lauded, do not showcase the original thinking of the Founders; instead they are a carved monument to political cynicism.

The anti-Federalists were like a group of children on a trip to the playground, who, when shown a sign that says "no hitting, pushing, or wrestling,

but otherwise have fun" then ask that the sign include a specific set of guarantees such as 1. Kids are allowed to slide on the slides 2. Government shall
not abridge the right of kids to swing on the swing-sets, etc. The kids could
already slide and swing, and the American people would have possessed
rights to free speech and all the rest without ten added amendments.

Madison's Tenth Amendment states, in fancy 18th century verbiage, that
if a specific right is not listed in the Constitutional Amendments then the
right to decide whether the people have that right is left up to the people or
the states. In other words, if the Constitution does not forbid it, then assume
that it can be done until the states pass a law forbidding it. Of course, the
Constitution remains silent about a lot of things (speed limits and marriage
laws, for example) and slavery was one of them. This meant, in practice, that
the Constitution left laws regarding slavery up to the states.

Only after the Civil War, when the Fourteenth Amendment passed, did the
courts determine that the First Amendment, which only says that "Congress
shall make no law," somehow applied to state governments as well. This is
a little chink in Constitutional law that never has been adequately explained
with logic, except that the courts and federal government assumed a power
they intended to keep.

At least the first flaw to the Constitution had a clear remedy: a Constitutional ban on slavery, even if it took winning a Civil War to achieve the aim.
The Constitution's second flaw, that neither Madison nor any of the other
Founders could foresee the influence of political parties, requires more creative thinking.

Madison cannot be accused of lacking political instinct; he logically understood that a Constitution was better than no Constitution, and even though
the version that was eventually ratified contained much less centralized force
than he envisioned, he understood that the status quo was a confederacy of
colonies/quasi-states that had hitherto possessed localized power. He got the
best Constitution he could.

However, Madison may have been inflicted by the traditional scholar's
curse: an inability to understand how raw human nature can rough up pure
philosophy. Schooled in the classics, and treating Montesquieu and his
separation of powers concept as foundational, Madison could not foresee the
vulgar development of political parties. Washington was too clear of a choice
for the first person to preside (hence, "president") over a Constitutional re-
public and he needed no party. This meant that the Founders ratified a Constitution that contained no defense against party politics. And, given that the
people who are elected to Congress and the executive branch all profess an

allegiance to a party, the likelihood of an anti-party Amendment ever being passed would seem small.

The thinking of the Constitution's Framers had been shaped by the Glorious Revolution, and they tended to fear that an executive could overpower the elected legislative body. Political theorists tend to react, or overreact, to the most recent threat, and not see that this can leave them vulnerable to unseen problems. In this sense, the Founders were much like Woodrow Wilson, Georges Clemenceau, and Lloyd George, the three men at the Paris Peace Conference of 1919 who focused so much on trying to contain Communism that they failed to anticipate the threat of fascism. (They were like boxers who focused too much on avoiding their opponent's left, and left themselves open to a hard right.) With their focus on avoiding tyranny from above, the Founders failed to see the threat of party politics from below.

What is the problem with party politics? The foremost problem is that it makes politics into falsely binary system. Consider the 2018 race for a senate seat in Texas that featured the liberal Democrat Beto O' Rourke versus the conservative Republican Ted Cruz. O' Rourke won 48.3% of the vote and Cruz received 50.9%. Over 48% of the Texans who voted in that election preferred a liberal Democrat yet, with Cruz, Texas will now put a senator in the Congress who will vote with conservative Republicans at or near 100% of the time. This type of scenario occurs in various political locales for various offices across the country; political parties create a falsely binary system of politics.

Does this lead to the problems of civics, cynicism, and apathy that mark the current era of federal politics? There is no way to determine this, but elected officials in "safe" districts or states might go further left or right given that they know they will pay a penalty for not voting with their faction for 100% of the time (a primary challenger can always promise to go further left or right) and a Democrat in a Republican district might simply decide to opt out of politics entirely, since her views, even if represented by a sizeable minority, will never find any political support. Again, this was not a considered part of the original vision for the Constitution; it is a result of the Founders not foreseeing the creation of parties.

At this point, let us return to this chapter's original thought experiment. What if someone ran for Congress with just one idea, that she would allow her constituents to vote on a secure website to answer the question about how often she (the congressperson) should vote with Republicans?

No system is without disadvantages, and the big problem with her platform is that the congresswoman will not be carefully reading legislation and voting on it based on its merits like all of her congressional colleagues (ha!). Also, this system divides up the role of a House representative into 1. Voting and 2. Creating legislation based on the needs of the constituency. It is possible that she could craft a piece of legislation that her random vote generator would then tell her to vote against, which would be weird but not catastrophic.

The advantages of the system are that, at least for her constituents, the binary system of party politics would be broken. She could truly claim to be representing the political leanings of the people in her district. Here's the best part: if someone got mad at either the Democrats or Republicans there would be no need at all to vote her out. The next time, just adjust the percentage that you want her to vote with the Republicans either up or down. This plan corrects a long-standing disjunction in American politics.

What would happen, you might ask, if every politician in the country did this? It would not be possible to have such a system if parties went away entirely. In that unlikely event, we would then have to restructure politics again, but without Democrats or Republicans entirely. New thought experiments might fill that need.

This leads to another point about elections, voting, and public perceptions. How should a citizen decide how to vote? One might answer that very few people put a lot of thought into elections and, given that voter turnout is higher in presidential election years, the electorate as a whole cannot discern what offices actually matter. The presidential election usually affects average people less than city council, school board, or mayoral elections, and yet voters tend to show the least interest in those.

Even in presidential elections there seems to be no clear standard for why it would be better to vote for one person over another. 2016's Clinton vs. Trump (they seemed to blend together at times, into a single Clump) set a modern standard for electoral nastiness. In October of 2012, Mitt Romney began his debate against Barack Obama by wishing the president and his wife a happy anniversary; America seemingly went from the Andy Griffith Show to splatterhouse horror-porn in just four years in terms of televised rhetoric by what standard should someone vote?

Rationalists can make a case for voting around a single issue. As president, a rationalist would want you to invade zero countries. All of the best presidents invade zero countries and all of the worst presidents invade more than zero countries. Domestic issues, tax rates, health care, education, etc., all appear to bureaucratic sinks that simply absorb reform attempts; elected heads of bureaucracies serve short terms whereas the middle managers in the system work for life, so nothing ever changes much. If given extra money, bureaucracies create more bureaucracy and find ways to redirect money toward waste.

In general, a "president" is analogous to a circus ringmaster; he is the only person without a special talent and so he declares himself the master of the ceremonies, even though the show could easily go on without him. Presidents, like CEOs, coaches, school principals, etc., really cannot do anything good, but they can create damage, which is why a "good" president, like any good leader, should be judged by the least amount of damage done.

Also, it seems like discrepancies over something like tax policy or health care should not be assigned the same amount of weight as the act of killing someone in another country. Here are three core reasons why the only criteria that we should hold a presidential candidate to is the likelihood that this president will invade another country:

1. Because of the constrained nature of the presidential office, presidents can only really create extreme levels of damage by invading other countries. Bad legislation, like Bush's No Child Left Behind, Obamacare, or Reagan's tax cuts, don't accomplish much but hassle for the bureaucracies and general inconvenience. However, presidents can actually kill a lot of people and waste a lot of money by invading other countries. On the high end of estimates, for example, about two million Vietnamese died in the chaos of the Vietnam War. To use another case, it's been estimated that about 460,000 Iraqis have died since the 2003 U.S. invasion.
2. If we count all human life as equal, then we might imagine how Americans would have reacted if the Bush administration had ordered an invasion of Wyoming, a state with a population of 544,270. Counting a one-to-one death rate, this hypothetical invasion of Wyoming would have subsequently led to the butchering of 84.5% of the state's population. Since I do not consider the lives of Wyoming's residents to be of more or less importance than those of people living in Iraq, and because the invasion of Iraq created the same amount of positives (that would be none) that an invasion of Wyoming would have, I'm going to count the real invasion of Iraq as equivalent to an invasion of Wyoming. After all, Wyoming and Iraq had the same number of weapons of mass destruction.
3. It would be interesting to ask how much an American citizen would be willing to save the life of someone from Wyoming. Would it be worth $5,217,391 per life? That's how much we spent, per corpse, to kill 460,000 Iraqis. Wouldn't it also be interesting if the American government (which is the people's government, since we pay for it) got *paid* $5,217,391 dollars for every Iraqi killed; even then the invasion would be a bad idea. However, not invading Iraq would have saved 460,000 lives at the equivalent of $5,217,391 per person. Imagine a piece of legislation that

saved the lives of 460,000 people and brought in over five million dollars for every person saved! *That is precisely the good deal that not invading other countries brings in for Americans.*

As a senator, Hillary Clinton voted for the Iraqi invasion. Trump, in a 2016 South Carolina primary debate, said this to the brother (if you can't remember, his name is JEB!) of George W. Bush: "Everything that's happening started with us stupidly going into the war in Iraq . . . and people talk about me with the button. I'm the one that doesn't want to do this, okay?" That statement, coupled with Trump's "America First" rhetoric (code for not sending the military into the business of foreign countries) might make Trump the best candidate for a pacifist.

Yes, that meant voting for mean tweets, casual racism, a badly-planned tax cut, a ditz for Education secretary, a trade war with China, conservative appellate judges, and, worst of all, the detention and separation of refugee families on the southern border of the United States. Still, it's been estimated that 24 immigrants have died in U.S. custody. This is inexcusable, but quite a different number from the 460,000 who died in the Iraq War sanctioned by G. W. Bush and Hillary Clinton. Based on her record, a voter might see no reason to believe that less than 24 people would have died as a result of presidential policy during a Clinton presidential tenure.

Here's the thing; we can weight presidential decisions in the same way that teachers can weight grades. This is all subjective, of course, but a "mean tweet" might be in a category weighted at .000001%, while a policy that can be said to lead directly to the death of someone (American or otherwise) can be rated at .90. Imagine weighting all of the decisions that a president makes in this manner, with, say health care legislation as a .2, and you can get some idea of how a president's total tenure can be judged by mathematical terms.

Again, the only real power that a president has to affect change is to launch a military strike on some place or another, so therefore the judicious use of such authority should be the major consideration of any voter. Trump's "America First" rhetoric, in some ways, meant that the United States will seek to preserve the lives of its soldiers and its wealth by, get ready for it, *not invading other countries.*

Political thought experiments that are designed to correct Constitutional flaws actually have a long history. The electoral college originally came into being as a way of increasing the influence of slaveholders who wanted the Three-Fifths Clause that gave them the "slave power" over Congressional elections to be additionally influential over the presidential elections. In presidential elections, this means 50 separate presidential elections rather than one big one, and, as everyone knows, whether a candidate wins a state by a single vote or by one million, the payoff is just the same.

Few people like this archaic system, and it effectively buries the votes of Democratic voters in conservative states and vice-versa for conservative voters in Democratic states. Yet Constitutional amendments are too hard to pass and the representatives of states that benefit from the Electoral College are reluctant to change it. Indiana Senator Birch Bayh (1928–2019) came up with a state-by-state plan whereby each state could pass legislation that would require the electors to throw their support behind whoever won the popular vote. There are 538 electors and a candidate needs 270 to win the presidency, so not all states would have to pass legislation, just 270 electoral votes worth.

It's an interesting solution, but, like climate change, the federal electoral college seems to be an overall problem and not a local problem. State-elected officials and their appointed bureaucrats do not, generally, receive accolades or votes for trying to solve national problems and, so, the incompatibilities continue on.

Thought experiments regarding politics tend to get interrupted by reality, but a teacher who raises such questions encourages students to study political history with a new purpose. In turn, this might encourage students or others who are interested in the political history of the country to think more deeply about the origins of our political structures.

In particular, the widespread misunderstanding of what the Declaration of Independence with its "All men are created equal" phrase actually means indicates that most historical and political commentators simply misunderstand how historical documents must be read with the original audience in mind. Such a problem recurs consistently in the process of historical scholarship.

KEY POINTS AND CLASSROOM APPLICATION

- Political parties were not envisioned by the authors of the United States Constitution. England's 1688 Glorious Revolution, which featured the development of parliamentary control over the sovereign, was the model. The thinking was that the Congress would put checks on the power of the president, but political parties have twisted that original intent.
- The notion that "All Men are created equal" likely represented Jefferson's attempt to develop a philosophical base that differed from that of the "Divine Right of Kings" philosophy. It was probably not an attempt to make broad statement about humanity's rights.

- The current political structure is accidentally binary in the sense that 51% of the people might vote for a candidate who will then vote cast conservative or liberal votes 100% of the time. A candidate who promises to allow constituents to vote on a secure website on the question of "how often do you want me to vote with the Republicans?" would fix this problem.
- Politics may not be the best place for logic.

Chapter Five

Risk, Odds, Bravery, and Ethics

In 2018, National Geographic released a documentary film titled *Free Solo* that featured Alex Honnold, a gifted cliff-face climber in his early thirties, and his attempts to climb the sheer El Capitan (El Cap). El Cap is a natural granite structure in Yosemite National Park in California that stretches upward from the ground to about 3,000 feet. Lots of climbers go up El Cap, but they do so with safety harnessing. Honnold made it a personal goal to climb the face of the rock without any safety equipment. After a certain height, any small slip would kill him.

The movie creates a series of ethical questions that connect with each other, but it should be stated that, as any thinking person can surmise from the fact that the movie was distributed, Honnold did make the climb without safety equipment and that he obviously did not fall. The movie garnered several awards, raised Honnold's celebrity profile, and presumably made some money for the grounded filmmakers.

Alex Honnold is an imbecile, of course, a product of a "personal best" culture that lauds young people for achieving pointless athletic or academic aims. A lot of Honnold's motivation seemed to be explained, at one point in the movie, when it was mentioned that he was an International Baccalaureate student in high school; this is where young people learn to impress their elders by mastering meaningless skills. Watching the movie brings up three thoughts, listed here in order of importance:

1. Climbing El Capitan without safety gear was no "achievement." The most disturbing moments in the movie are not when Honnold climbs the cliff face, but when he finishes and the viewer realizes that nothing has been

achieved at all. A few moments after reaching the top; Alex is back in his van and continuing on with his exercise routine.

2. Honnold resembles nothing so much as a video game character who is attempting a tough level with only one life. Is this the appeal of these adventure activities?

3. The movie could not have been made without Honnold's adorable girl-friend, Sanni McCandless. Several years younger than Alex, she cries and worries and wonders why. This creates two appealing features to the movie, the first being that it puts Alex into the masculine position of going out on a dangerous quest while his damsel waits on him. Second, it gives Alex's life value (his mother is strangely passive about her son's reckless-ness), as we want Alex to survive, if only to spare Sanni pain.

Now, on to the thought experiments. How reckless does an action have to be before it is just stupid and/or evidence of mental illness? What if a young man became obsessed with the idea of playing Russian Roulette and wanted to put one bullet in a six-shooter? Would a documentary film crew follow him around, put a camera in his crying girlfriend's face, and then end the film with him pulling a trigger next to his head? Would the "click" of an empty chamber be just as glorious as Alex reaching the top of El Cap?

Let's examine the similarities and differences between climbing El Cap "free solo" and playing a game of Russian Roulette:

Similarities: 1. A risk to life; 2. an obsession about risking one's life; 3. attention-seeking; 4. emotional manipulation of loved ones (how nice it must be to see how much one is loved); and 5. no purpose at all to the risk.

Difference: 1. Playing Russian Roulette requires almost no skill whereas climbing El Capitan is something that only a small number of people can do.

If the only difference is the level of skill involved, then we can imagine a scenario where, say, a gifted pianist decides to play Mozart while suspended over a tank of hungry crocodiles. If he misses a note, a trapdoor opens and he gets chomped. If our gifted pianist suggested such a shenanigan, where would it be legal? Should the people around him look to make a buck off this idea, or should they suggest that the pianist get mental help for having suicidal thoughts?

In fact, you can take any specialized skill and imagine a person putting himself into a position where a small failure will cause bodily harm or death and create an exact analogy with Alex Honnold's climbing actions. This brings up another point; Alex is a male and I have used masculine pronouns here when describing hypothetical individuals. What if we reversed the situation and put the cute girlfriend, Sanni, up on El Capitan and put Alex in the van where he could sit and cry?

That's right. What if Sanni decided to free solo El Cap, and the camera crew interviewed a worried Alex and talked to Sanni's father (as opposed to Alex's mother) about her adventure? How would we feel then? Would Nat Geo had filmed this? Would Yosemite's park officials have been so chill about a violation of park rules and (probably) federal law? Risking one's life is a masculine virtue, not a feminine one. Does that matter?

The reason that Alex Honnold was allowed to climb El Cap, and was allowed to make money off of what amounts to an attempted suicide (*Free Solo* is a snuff film with a happy ending), is because the public filed Honnold's scaling attempt into a sports analogy column rather than a mental illness column.

In some ways, the obvious analogy is to compare Honnold to a circus tightrope walker, the point of the circus being to heighten the sense of anxiety in the audience as someone with specialized skills engages in a "death-defying" stunt. Yet, the difference is that Honnold had only a small live audience and most of us who watched his rock-face ascent did so in the comfort of a seat, already knowing the outcome.

For the purpose of trying to inject some meaning into their activities, extreme athletes often either try to collect money for charities or they justify their actions with some vague paeon to "inspiration," meaning that people who watch the athlete might be inspired to do something great as well. In 2014, "The Iron Cowboy" James Lawrence, a forty-something triathlete from Texas, completed 50 Iron Man length triathlons in 50 states in 50 days.

This is impressive work, not overtly dangerous in the way that climbing a cliff face without a harness is, and utterly pointless. Interviews reveal Lawrence to be a likeable man, and he seems to be dedicated to his wife and many children, but what is the purpose of the triathlons? The obligatory answer: to inspire people to engage in fitness activities.

Okay, fine, and that may be okay for swimming, biking, and running. But what is Honnold inspiring? Rock climbing is not the kind of fitness activity that most people can regularly engage in. In June of 2018, not long after the release of *Free Solo*, two climbers with safety gear died trying to ascend El Cap. One was named Tim Klein, who was a gifted high school teacher with a wife and children. Klein had climbed El Cap dozens of times, but on this day an accident occurred that killed him and a friend. A year later, a teacher's aide in her late fifties died on El Cap.

All told, five people have died on El Cap, and three of those after the release of *Free Solo*. In November of 2019, Honnold was on the rock face again, this time with safety gear and the company of a 33-year-old climber named Emily Harrington. Emily fell, received a concussion and several other injuries, and became the damsel in distress to Honnold's knight. The media treated Honnold as a hero for helping to prevent Harrington from dying, but is it heroism to create the conditions of danger and then rescue oneself or someone else from those conditions?

Here's the problem: we don't have a clear definition of "heroism" because the term itself usually is only applied in a manipulative manner. Military personnel, for example, are routinely called heroes even if the technological disparity in firepower between, say, an American Marine Corps Unit and a group of terrorist fighters is greater than that of 19th century British forces, armed with rapid-firing Maxim guns, and the African tribalists in the Sudan.

It's hard to see how there is any heroism in turning the crank on a Maxim Gun while mowing down African warriors who carry only spears, but somehow American soldiers with body armor, tanks, sci-fi level guns, and the ability to call in airstrikes get labeled as heroic for occupying the same neighborhoods that barefoot Iraqi children have to live in daily.

Yet, soldiers are labeled as "heroic" because they risk themselves, even if it is often a minimal risk, for a cause. Honnold faced more danger on El Cap than the average infantry soldier does in the Middle East, but Honnold served no greater purpose. Soldiers risk themselves for the greater good of a country, or that's the idea. What happens when the nation fights for no good purpose, or for destructive purposes, as was the case in Vietnam and Iraq?

The uneasy answer is that soldiers are not allowed to question the nature of the mission, only to perform their duties on command. This means that the soldier cannot question the overall ideals of the mission, and this means that soldiers fight for no greater purpose at all, which means that heroism is not a part of any military action.

For cases such as this, an extreme analogy can be useful for illuminating the reasoning. Imagine a soldier in a control room staring at a screen. She controls a drone that flies over a village in Afghanistan and drops bombs on a terrorist enclave. Her actions cannot be described as heroic because she is at no personal risk.

Killing terrorists might be a good thing, and therefore a higher purpose might be served, but the lack of personal risk means that she is no hero. How close to danger would she need to be before her actions become heroic? Would she need to call in the airstrike while being in the village herself?

Likewise, an American soldier stationed in Iraq, who wears body armor and carries high powered weaponry, is living in the exact same conditions as your average Iraqi child, who must confront those conditions without any of the protections of the American soldier. How can we give medals for valor to U.S. soldiers without also giving medals for valor to every single average Iraqi? Of course, no one wants to ask these types of philosophical questions and so patriotic "Thank you for your service" mantras get shouted, almost frantically, to keep anyone from even beginning to probe them.

Heroism can never be framed as intellectual dissent or the ability to stand up to corrupt or illogical authorities—it must always be defined as the ability to risk bodily harm on behalf of a corporate entity.

Now, let's say that someone really wanted to call Honnold a hero for his rock climbing, or U.S. soldiers heroic for their occupying. What would a sophistic argument be? How is Honnold's free solo climb of El Cap any different from Neil Armstrong and Buzz Aldrin (or any of the subsequent astronauts) walking on the moon? The 1969 moon landing gets almost universally lauded as a great achievement not just for the United States but also for science; Armstrong and Aldrin usually get defined as American heroes. Criticisms of the moon landing typically come from leftists who were concerned about the costs of NASA, with the major claim being that the money for something like a moon landing might be better spent on social welfare programs.

The 1969 moon landing receives acclamation almost across the spectrum; the original astronauts get praised by history and celebrated in popular culture. However, no one has ever really been able to articulate why human beings were put on the moon in 1969, or in the subsequent moon missions. When President Kennedy, in March of 1962, first announced plans to put a man on the moon, he was giving a speech to a crowd at Rice University in Texas. The president did decide to try and answer the philosophical question of "why" with this phrase:

> But why, some say, the Moon? Why choose this as our goal? And they may well ask, why climb the highest mountain? Why, 35 years ago, fly the Atlantic? Why does Rice play Texas?

Other than everything George W. Bush said, these may be the stupidest lines ever uttered by a president. JFK poses some good questions: climbing the highest mountain, flying the Atlantic in a sub-par airplane, and playing football can all be described as dangerously pointless and wasteful activities. What good came from Hillary's ascent of Everest? In 2018, eleven people died on the overcrowded mountain trying to attain the summit, and for what?

Lindbergh may have flown across the Atlantic and made himself a hero, but did this improve his character or change the trajectory of aviation at all? Commercial flights across the Atlantic would have eventually occurred without Lindbergh, and the man used his fame to throw support toward the Nazis. JFK's invocation of the Rice versus Texas game is just more evidence that sports metaphors indicate the shallowest of thought processes. We would all be fine, and probably quite better off, if Rice never played Texas at all.

When asked about the necessity of the NASA moon missions, defenders of the Apollo programs either take the JFK "climb it because it's there" tack, or they argue that the moon missions created some kind of residual scientific achievement; the technologies developed for the missions had positive effects elsewhere. None of this quite makes sense in light of the actual history.

To begin with, when the Soviets launched *Sputnik* in 1957, this was seen by the Soviet power structure as a side diversion practiced by the Russian "Chief Designer" Sergei Kovolev (1907–1966). He was supposed to be designing rockets for military purposes but was personally fascinated with space travel. *Pravda* barely reported on the launch, but in the United States, Sputnik created a public fury.

Why did *Sputnik* provoke the American public in a way that, say, the Soviet detonation of a hydrogen bomb over Kazakhstan in 1953 did not? The answer probably has to do with another new technology: the television set. 1957 also happened to be the year that Elvis Presley swiveled his hips (an act deemed too obscene to be recorded by CBS's cameras) on the Ed Sullivan show.

For a brief period in American history, just about every middle class American household had access to just a few television programs, and this provided an opportunity for large-scale cultural phenomena that could not exist before in the era of radio and cannot exist now in the era of multiple channels and internet entertainment options.

Sputnik came at the perfect time for television news and even though the satellite possessed no immediate military purpose, the sober scientists and journalists who spoke to millions of Americans in black and white assured the American public that *Sputnik* was evidence of Soviet military supremacy. President Eisenhower, who had been concerned with Soviet rocket and bomb capabilities, rightly saw *Sputnik* as harmless, but his private views on the matter soon got overwhelmed by a public panic that turned into a public demand.

A thorough study of the "space race" is not needed here, but it should be enough to say that Khrushchev found the American attention to be flattering and, like all bureaucrats everywhere (especially so in the Soviet state), he rushed in to take credit for something he was surprised to find had happened. In September of 1959, the Soviets crashed the Luna 2 spacecraft onto the Moon and might be said to have "won" the race with that action. A few months later the Soviets photographed the far side of the Moon.

The United States government inadvertently started redefining the race at that point by pulling up the stakes of the finish line and putting them further and further from Soviet achievements. Kennedy was no physicist; his grandiose statement in 1962 at Rice University was probably just hyperbole. If we put his statement into a statistical column with lots of other presidential promises, his would be one of a handful that randomly got accomplished. It's worth remembering that G. W. Bush, in a January 2004 speech, announced that NASA should return people to the moon by 2020 and then start planning missions to Mars (more on that in a moment.)

In practice, what the idea of putting astronauts on the moon did was this: it increased the weight of the rockets. By 1962, both the Soviets and Americans were launching rockets into space using oxygen-infused kerosene as fuel. Both sides were putting carbon-based materials (dogs, chimpanzees, and humans) into orbit for no scientific reason. There are only two possible reasons why any carbon-based material needed to be on the rockets or in the satellites at all:

1. All of the missions up until the 1969 moon landing were preparatory for putting people on the Moon. Like all big achievements, this had to be achieved in increments.
2. The carbon-based material in the rockets, on both the Soviet and American sides, put something of value at risk.

This is an interesting thought experiment: could the Soviets have achieved the same effect in 1961 had they sent a Faberge egg or early copy of *War and Peace* or Lenin's corpse into orbit instead of Yuri Gagarin? If Gagarin's only function was to show how confident the Soviets were in their spaceflight abilities, so confident that they would put useless human cargo on board just to enhance the risk, then why wouldn't a valuable inanimate object work instead?

Instead of sending Scott Carpenter into orbit in response, the United States could have put an early copy of the Constitution, or a billion dollars in cash, or some treasure from the Smithsonian into a rocket and then sent that into orbit around the Earth. Probably the use of pilots gave the NASA missions a military connotation; or it could be (said with a wink) that in the 1950s and 1960s that the most valued commodity in the U.S. were short-haired white males.

Nonetheless, the decision to send human beings on a moon mission eventually allowed the U.S. to set a goal that the Soviets could not achieve. But this was not something planned from the beginning; the moon landing was a byproduct of defensive goals.

In order to understand the 1969 moon landing, we have to go back to 1942, which was the year that the Nazis launched the V-2 rocket. The head scientist of that program, a verdant Nazi named Werner Von Braun (1912–1977), would eventually be captured by the American military and would be assigned, as a POW of sorts, the role of lead rocket designer. Of course, at the same time that Von Braun was creating the V-2 rockets, the scientists involved in the Manhattan Project were busying themselves developing the atomic bombs that eventually liquidated huge sections of both Hiroshima and Nagasaki in Japan in 1945.

It is not unusual for historians, most of whom are not also physicists, to misunderstand the importance of the atomic bombing of Japan. The importance of the detonations was not so much in the actual destruction of the cities, as ordinary firebombing, it is often remarked, could be more destructive to life and property.

The importance of the atomic bombs was in the potentiality for creating nuclear fission bombs. In 1941, Takutaro Hagiwara, a Japanese physicist, published a paper where he predicted that an atomic explosion would be hot enough to fuse hydrogen into one of its isotopes, deuterium, and that would create an explosion that would be the equivalent of a miniature sun. A nuclear explosion could then be turned into a thermonuclear explosion.

After 1945, two separate defensive races took off between the U.S. and the Soviet Union. The first race was to create a hydrogen bomb, and the second race involved creating a convergence between thermonuclear weapons and long-distance rockets. Whoever turned a bomb, dropped from the belly of a bulky plane, into a warhead that could be attached to the tip of a rocket would possess the ability to launch thermonuclear strikes on the enemy from a secure location that was far enough away that a retaliatory strike could be avoided.

In 1952, the American military, with a horrifying recklessness that should have condemned the entire chain-of-command concept, exploded a hydrogen bomb in the South Pacific. In the same year, Von Braun published a paper that set forth plans for how a rocket could reach space. A year later, the Soviets successfully tested a hydrogen bomb over Kazakhstan. With thermonuclear explosions going off at the same time that the Korean War entered a stalemate, actual space exploration seemed a distant concern.

Then, in 1957, Sputnik accidentally changed that. From that point forward, the Soviets and Americans needed to find a proxy way to show off their long-distance rocket capability without actually bringing about a nuclear end-times. (Hydrogen bombs are actually not quite as destructive as are often portrayed; because the explosion rises, it can only reach about a ten-mile radius before it pushes a chunk of the atmosphere into space. Make the bomb one thousand times stronger and it just rises ten thousand times faster—nothing can increase the blast diameter. It's the DNA-tearing fallout that does the long-term damage; this is why the Soviet-American arms race was about numbers rather than size.)

After *Sputnik*, the Soviets held a steady lead in the achievements of space "exploration" (so-called) until 1967. Sergei Kovelev died during a botched stomach operation in 1966, but his death did not cause the Soviet decline. Rather, the Chief Designer died knowing that the United States would send astronauts to the Moon in a way that the U.S.S.R could not. Von Braun now planned to move away from the Mercury Redstone rockets that had been staples of the U.S. rocket program and towards a new Saturn model. The Saturn rockets were big enough to be able to tow the kind of life-sustaining apparatus that would be needed to keep people alive on a trip to the moon.

However, the Saturn rockets required a new kind of fuel, liquid hydrogen, to achieve liftoff. Kerosene would no longer do. Kovelev knew that the Soviets could not just build bigger rockets to keep up with the Americans, as the now-antiquated Soviet rocket fuel would rattle a bigger rocket apart.

Alas, the Soviet *apparatchiks* never understood the physics, and nothing in Lenin's writings were any help on the matter, and so the orders were given to upscale the rockets without improving the fuel, and one Soviet rocket after another exploded on the launch pad.

After 1967, the United States had created all of the scientific components for a Moon landing. The question, then, is this: why actually put people on the Moon? 1967 was also the year that the Apollo 1 disaster killed Gus Grissom and his crew on the ground, demonstrating the dangers inherent in space travel. Why couldn't the United States have just sent a Saturn rocket, complete with the weight of the life-giving apparatus and three dummies filled with sandbags, to the moon instead of three astronauts?

The moon landing was not necessary to prove a theory; one could say that the physics for putting a person on the Moon had been established in 1687 by Isaac Newton and the Inverse Square Law (gravity gets weaker as one gets further from the center of the heavy object). One would have to say that Newton's theories were pretty well proven by the 1960s.

The Moon Landing should be best understood as an engineering feat, with the United States creating the rocket and rocket fuel necessary to tow modules with the capacity to keep astronauts alive in space and on the Moon.

But, once everything had been built, what was the purpose of actually sending Armstrong, Aldrin, and Collins all the way up there? Or for that matter, sending astronauts around the moon as had been the case with the Apollo 8 mission, or sending anyone out on a "spacewalk" while in orbit around the Earth?

The moon landing mission itself might even be considered kind of a joke; someone might misconstrue Armstrong as being subjected to the big three psychological tortures. After all, the mission involved a confined space (claustrophobia), being shot up into orbit (fear of heights), and then, when Armstrong finally stepped onto the moon he found himself having to give a speech to essentially everyone on the planet (fear of public speaking).

The only two compelling scientific reasons to send people to the Moon can easily be dispelled.

1. The astronauts brought back moon rocks that helped to determine the age of the moon. Great. First of all, those are some expensive rocks. Secondly, the Soviets gathered rocks mechanically a year later in 1970 with the Luna 16 mission. Does anyone doubt that if the money, time, and energy that NASA had spent on the manned mission had been redirected to a mechanical mission to collect moon rocks, the U.S. could not have brought back rocks in a different way?
2. NASA's moon mission, by proxy, created new technologies that provided benefits in other areas of science and engineering. Again, fine, but that technology was established before the astronauts actually got launched, so the same things would have been achieved by just leaving the Saturn rocket on the ground.

And here we return to our *Free Solo* comparison: the only logical reason that anyone can give for putting human beings on the moon is that such an act inspires humans to achieve. Achieve what? Wrapping a pointless and dangerous activity up in science makes the risk no less stupid at its core. Alex Honnold climbing to the top of El Cap and Neil Armstrong stepping onto the moon both achieved nothing of importance at all. Putting yourself into a condition of danger in the hope that this will demonstrate how impressive your skills are or your technology is cannot be described as either brave or inspirational, but merely reckless.

As was mentioned earlier, three people have died on El Cap since *Free Solo*'s release and another woman was seriously injured while on the rock face with Honnold himself. In contrast, 17 astronauts lost their lives in the NASA missions, three in the Apollo 1 disaster, seven in the 1986 Challenger explosion, and seven more in the 2003 Columbia explosion that occurred during atmospheric re-entry. NASA has launched about two hundred "manned" missions, so to have two of those that were in flight end in disaster means that they have a horrific failure rate of 1%.

As of 2018, commercial aircraft average 0.36 deaths for every *million* flights, meaning that someone dies on a large commercial aircraft once every three million flights. NASA has killed 14 people in two hundred flights (not counting the Apollo 1), which means that one person dies for about every 14 takeoffs. For what? Inspiration?

Despite all of this, NASA scientists and various politicians and science commentators continue to reference the idea of putting astronauts on Mars, and perhaps not just for inspirational purposes but also to explore the idea of human settlement there. Ignorance, usually, is behind these statements. It took NASA's Curiosity rover 253 days to get to Mars, whereas the trip to the Moon takes about three days.

Mars is the next closest thing out there, but to say that we can send astronauts there is about like a man who walked from Bangor, Maine to Philadelphia, Pennsylvania assuming that he can probably also walk to Tokyo, Japan.

Some science articles have discussed how the mental health of astronauts going to Mars might be affected by the trip. It would mean 253 days in a confined space, followed by the arrival on a hostile planet, a long stay (if one is to wait for Mars and Earth to get close enough together to make the return trips shorter), and then another long trip back. It has been suggested by scientists and science fiction writers that the astronauts might be put to sleep for the trip's duration.

Even upon arrival, it's not as if Mars is going to treat the Earthlings with hospitality; Earth's magnetosphere shields us from most harmful radiation and Mars doesn't have one. Humans who make it to the Red Planet would immediately either have to build lead dwellings or dig underground.

We already can send space rovers there that safely send back information about Mars (this is all justified by human curiosity regarding the solar system, but there's a price tag associated with satisfying that curiosity). This all brings up an important question: "Why?" If all we are going to do is sleep on the way to Mars and dig underground when we get there, then why not stay home and try to clean this planet up?

The answer is simple: neither NASA nor any other entity is ever going to send human beings to Mars. The costs, logistics, and risk make the mission nearly impossible and, even if it became possible, pointless. This is not like Columbus's 1492 expedition; he didn't know what was out there. We know what is on Mars and we know what is between us and Mars.

Why, then, is the idea so prevalent? Well, the idea itself, given to a largely uninformed public, is worth money. Preachers give fiery sermons all the time about an Armageddon that never arrives, but the money is not in the event but in the excitement generated about the event.

This brings us back to our thought analogy—is Alex Honnold like a NASA astronaut? Yes, both engaged in pointless risks that, however, ended up enriching certain entities because the public was enraptured by the risk, and then sold the idea that the risk was worth it for "inspirational" reasons. One suspects that if the cameras had been off, then Honnold would have stayed grounded, and one further suspects that if the public were more scientifically literate, then talk of a human landing on Mars would dissipate.

The difference between Honnold and an astronaut might be in the skill level. NASA created strict educational and physical requirements for the first set of astronauts and also imposed physical and psychological testing on them (the tests provided the most memorable sections of both the book and movie versions of Tom Wolfe's *The Right Stuff*) but the reasons for this were never clear.

Ultimately, the astronauts were just expected to sit in a confined space. The requirements and testing, however, gave the appearance to the public that some special skill was needed to be an astronaut, thus creating a sense of exclusivity.

Honnold's rock-face ascent required real physical skills far more impressive than being strapped into a seat. This high skill level may be what separates his free solo ascent from any other bizarre endeavor as the positive good to society might be the general inspiration of other people to do great things. Yet, this argument makes little sense either, because the danger that Honnold put himself in was, like that of the astronauts, completely unnecessary.

Again, imagine a concert-level pianist who wants to play a virtuoso piece while suspended over a tank of unfed crocodiles; one wrong note triggers a trapdoor that will drop her into the jaws of the carnivores below her. Should she be allowed to do this? Does the threat of impending death make her skills more impressive and, thus more inspirational? No, the whole conceit reeks of absurdity and illegality. If a friend of mine suggested she might do this, then I would likely suggest she could benefit from psychiatric help. Honnold's "friends" apparently grabbed a camera and found out how they could make money from it.

The topic of money and risk becomes even more interesting when applied to sports gambling, which is the most public and popular way in which mathematics gets applied. Sports betting is also the place where the Platonic nature of pure mathematics and the nature of the actual material world are shown to be at variance.

Extreme examples usually provide the best teaching tools. The most recent "extreme" example of the dichotomy between mathematical odds and sporting reality occurred on August 26, 2017, when all-time great boxer Floyd Mayweather entered into a pugilistic contest with the mixed martial artist Connor McGregor. McGregor made his pro debut as a boxer against a Hall of Fame fighter. The difference between their skill levels was significant enough that one seasoned boxing analyst, Max Kellerman, questioned whether it would be possible for McGregor to land even one punch.

Ordinarily in a top-level boxing match, both athletes would be close enough in their skill level that each would have to train hard and try to fight at their highest potential to win. In this case, however, the discrepancy between Mayweather and McGregor was so wide that Mayweather could decide how and when he wanted to end the fight. In sports betting, small factors can alter the potential outcome of an event. If that knowledge is not widely shared, then those who have insider access to it can more accurately assess the odds of probable outcomes than those who lack the insider knowledge.

Of course, the more variables that are added to an event, the harder the event is to predict. A basketball game is less "fixable" than a boxing match. In the case of Mayweather vs. McGregor, it was possible for Mayweather to decide ahead of time that he was going to carry his opponent into the tenth round and then knock him out. If Mayweather dropped that information to his friends and relatives, and they chose to make bets based on that boasting, then who would know?

An equivalent event would involve some average weekend runner engaging in a 5-mile race with a professional marathoner. The odds would overwhelmingly be with the marathoner as some unlikely event like an injury or meteor strike would be required to prevent her victory. However, if bettors were allowed to pick the exact spot on the course where the marathoner would break away from the average runner, then this whole scenario would take on a different connotation. It's completely up to the marathoner when she decides to break away, and so if she decided to do that at the four mile marker rather than after 10 feet, that's her decision. If she decides to share that decision with some other people, then how is that cheating?

This becomes a question about intentions; is it always incumbent upon an athlete to do the absolute best that he or she can? If so, why? Is it just to prevent sports gamblers from having to worry about one more factor? In the case of Mayweather vs. McGregor, Mayweather could easily say that he carried the fight for 10 rounds to put on a show for everyone who paid for the fight, and that if you decided to bet on the fight, then you should know that he intended to put on a show.

Ultimately and ethically, the question becomes this: whether someone is risking death on El Cap, or risking concussions or worse in sporting events, why put a camera on the behavior and money on the table?

KEY POINTS

- Alex Honnold's free solo ascent of El Capitan in Yellowstone National Park sparks a thought experiment about the difference between recklessness and bravery. Why was he allowed to try something so dangerous and what was the purpose?
- By developing thought experiments around the subject of Honnold and his climb, we can then develop ethical parameters that can be applied to a variety of hypotheticals, but also to the reality of NASA's moon landings.
- The concept of bravery as applied to soldiers cannot be set outside the bounds of inquiry.
- Controlling the factors in a sporting event allows for the adjustment of odds, but should we be putting cameras on dangerous activities in any circumstance?

Chapter Six

Identity

To what extent should modern peoples feel connected to the historical groups they identify with? At first, this may seem to be the most examined question in the United States, but the underlying assumptions regarding identity politics remain largely thoughtless. The assumption being, for example, that African-Americans (however defined) are the current product of a history of slavery, post-Reconstruction oppression, and, in the modern era, institutional racism.

This narrative originated with African-Americans, but the conceit has spread to a variety of identity groups, including women, and is even and most unfortunately spreading to segments of the white population that define themselves as connected to a poorer rural community.

The question will come down to this: is racial or gender classification an arbitrary historical distinction, or is there a genuine connection to the history of a people? Let us imagine a person whose great-grandfather came to the United States from Prussia in 1869.

Should a person who learns this fact in his forties suddenly feel some connection with Prussia, learn the German language, and develop a grievance against the French and British for imposing unfair sanctions on Germany after the First World War?

What if this person did all of this, and then after a few years his mother called him up and said "Sorry, I was mistaken, your great-grandfather came over from Russia, not Prussia." Could this person keep proudly eating sauerkraut and extolling the virtues of Frederick the Great's enlightened rule, or would he then have to develop opinions about the Bolshevik execution of Czar Nicholas II?

The absurdity of such a stance regarding one's historical lineage is inherent to the process, and few Americans really care to develop a close connection with the "mother" country of their ancestors.

Still, this does not make the endeavor entirely unimportant; one might be able to trace certain cultural characteristics from a personal genealogy and understand certain words or family character traits that may have been passed down over generations and shaped our own character, but any attempt to define a specific historical class from such a genealogy dissolves into absurdity as one goes further back.

To connect this with the original conceit stated in this chapter is to pose two controversial thought experiment questions. In 1861, the first year of the American Civil War, the population of the United States totaled about 31 million people. At that time, the U.S. had four million slaves. The 2010 U.S. census stated that 42 million "non-hispanic" African-Americans lived in the U.S., and other sources indicate that 80% of those are culturally connected in some way to that original slave population.

The milder of the controversial questions then, is, after over 160 years, do African-Americans living now possess more of a connection to that population of four million slaves from 1861 than do any other peoples to their ancestral connections from the 1860s?

The second question here is more controversial. Would any African-American alive today want to change places, historically, with a slaveholder from 1861? This would mean, of course, giving up vaccinations, clean running water in the house, flush toilets, the internet, and all gas-powered vehicles, along with refrigeration, air conditioning, and every other modern convenience.

This question is dangerous because it leads us to a thought experiment that creates a more correct version of historical connection, one that pulls us away from racial or gender identifications. It's not dangerous to ask if any white person today would want to change places with a slave from 1861 because the answer is so obviously "no." Who would want to give up all of the modern conveniences of life in order to live under the oppressive conditions of southern slavery? However, asking the other question of African-Americans also brings up the same connotations, but has a more painful answer: life is better for African-Americans in the twenty-first century than it was for any population in the world in 1861, or, for that matter, in 1961.

Lest this seem like race-baiting, it should also be pointed out that American white people in the present who see connections to the antebellum south fall into the same type of thinking. Why should a white man in the 21st century feel any connection at all with a white person from the 1860s? Why not with a white woman, a black slave, or a Chinese immigrant? What's the direct connection between skin color today and skin color in the past?

Before explaining a better way to think, a detour into the history of this type of thinking will be useful and probably originated in 1848. In that year, Karl Marx and his benefactor Friedrich Engels published *The Communist Manifesto*, a pamphlet that funneled the human race into two categories: oppressor and oppressed. Marx identified the upper class as bourgeoisie, or those who owned the "means of production" (factory machinery) and the proletariat, those who worked on the machines and sold their time. In doing so, he linked each class to a long history of oppressors and oppressed, thus stretching the categories back into the medieval era so that the 19th century lower class as proletariat were invited to see themselves as connected to the 14th century peasants.

In that same year, a group consisting of 68 women and 32 men in Seneca Falls, New York, drafted the *Declaration of Sentiments*. Like the *Communist Manifesto*, the *Declaration* created a binary system for humanity. The authors transparently looked to the 1776 *Declaration of Independence* as their inspiration. This worked fine for the initial paragraphs, and the line "We hold these truths to be self-evident that all men and women are created equal . . ." coopts and expands an American ethos.

However, the analogy gets stretched too far after the preamble and philosophy. Jefferson's *Declaration* contained only a little philosophizing; the *Declaration* mostly consists of an itemized list of complaints against the king: evidence that the king (and England) had broken the social contract. But women's emancipation from a male-dominated system and a colony separating from a mother country are not analogous. This led to the binary system of thought that produced, in the *Declaration of Sentiments*, phrases such as these:

> The history of mankind is a history of repeated injuries and usurpations on the part of man toward woman, having in direct object the establishment of an absolute tyranny over her. To prove this, let facts be submitted to a candid world.
>
> He has not ever permitted her to exercise her inalienable right to the elective franchise. He has compelled her to submit to laws, in the formation of which she had no voice.

Compare this to Marx and Engels:

> The history of all hitherto existing society is the history of class struggles.
>
> Freeman and slave, patrician and plebian, lord and serf, guild-master and journeyman. In a word, oppressor and oppressed.

It might be surprising to see that the *Declaration of Sentiments* is more analogous to the *Communist Manifesto* than it is to the *Declaration of Independence* that the authors sought to mimic, but a binary system of oppressor and oppressed simply fits a female struggle for independence against men more aptly than does a colony separating from the mother country.

Binary systems are essentially Platonic, in the sense that they can operate only when there are clear and immutable categories: black and white, male and female, alive or dead, but these categories cannot deal with nuances.

Identity politics exist because people have the odd habit of assuming a connection to the past of their race, gender, and religious background. Imagine if "you" as you exist were put into a random shuffle and sent to a specific place and time; you might come out as anyone (remember the great 80s drama "Quantum Leap"?). How would this form your view of equality in society? Why would a white male in the 21st century identify only with white males from history?

Here are two questions:

1. Would we be comfortable with Denzel Washington playing Abraham Lincoln in a movie?
2. What about Paul Gianetti as Martin Luther King Jr.?

Neither role would involve either "white face" or "black face," the audience would know that the races of the actual historical characters are different from that played by the actor (audiences have had to use their imaginations before, like when Hamlet, a Dane, speaks English). Isn't the acting talent of the actor more important than the race of the character? Cate Blanchett played Bob Dylan in a movie once and was largely praised for the performance.

In early 2020, Barnes and Nobles booksellers released new covers of classics that featured more multicultural characters. Moby Dick's antagonist, Captain Ahab, was black on the cover (to use one example). This restructuring of the classics created such a scuttlebutt on social media that Barnes and Noble withdrew the covers. Why? No references are made to Ahab's skin tone in Moby Dick; who is to say that Ahab wasn't black? It's unlikely that Melville, during his writing process, imagined a black Ahab, but an author's intentions do not get to direct a reader's interpretation.

Identity politics leads to a strange logic, where people are invited to identify with the skin color, religious background, etc. of someone rather than with that person's interests or talents. Why should a black woman with no interest in reading or writing feel more of a connection with Toni Morrison than a white male who likes to read and write? Black History Month, Women's History Month, etc., are all built on that assumption.

This brings us to the thought experiment. Would your experience of reading or watching a play change at all if the race/gender/sexual orientation of the author was different from what you thought it was? For example, if scholars found compelling evidence that Shakespeare was a black woman, would we need to move the Shakespeare volumes into a new section of the library? Would the experience of reading or watching Shakespeare change at all based on this new information?

Conversely, what if turned out that Toni Morrison did not actually write either *Song of Solomon* (1977) or *Beloved* (1987), but instead that they were written by a Vietnamese woman? The experience of reading both books is moving in a literary way, and this new knowledge about Morrison's personal identity would make little difference in that experience.

The same is true of much feminist literature. For example, Caroline Criado Perez wrote a wonderful book titled *Invisible Women: Data Bias in a World Designed for Men* (2019), where she explained that vehicle safety standards, bathroom sizes, and cell phone sizes (among many other things) are built around a model that considers the average male to be the default. The book contains real data and, if it turned out that Caroline was actually a pseudonym for a male author, the experience of reading the book would not change. The insights gained from reading the book would not turn to ash upon discovering the author's real gender.

This is not true, however, of anything that Ta-Nehisi Coates has written. Coates won the National Book Award for *Between the World and Me* (2015), which is a letter to his son. Coates is a black man, and he also writes comic books and occasional pieces of journalism. If it turned out that Coates was actually a false front for a white man named Bob who lived in Arizona and looked like Dick Cheney, would the National Book Award committee (or the MacArthur Genius Award committee for that matter) merely shrug and say, "Well, it's only the writing that matters"?

Frustration with the public reception of Coates certainly got expressed in a 2017 podcast between two African-American intellectuals, Glenn Loury and John McWhorter. McWhorter is the author of several books (and a Great Courses lecture) in the field of linguistics. I had read several of his works and, because he has a name that's normally associated with white people, I assumed he was white.

The first time I realized he was black was when I listned to this podcast. This new knowledge about McWhorter's race did not change my appreciation of his books at all, but it was interesting to hear his views about Ta Nahesi-Coates. One wonders if Coates would possess all the awards he has if his name was John McWhorter.

Are there are other categories of oppressor and oppressed that can be created from history that go beyond the typical class, race, and gender classifications? I, for example, am a militant introvert. A forthcoming social gathering or work meeting conjures up at least three days, and often more, worth of dread in my stomach. Extroverted people, or even normally-verted people, never seem to know that we introverts exist.

And the pressure always seems to be exerted toward social gatherings. A holiday has never gone by where I was not asked to join a pitch-in lunch at work, or some equivalent, despite my persistent refusal. Conversely, I have never walked into a room full of people who are eating and talking during some social gathering and said, "Why don't you all go to a darkened room by yourselves and read some books?"

Other introverted people likely feel the same sense of persecution when it comes to social gatherings, and a couple of books have been written on the topic. Anneli Rusus's *Party of One* (2003) and *Quiet: The Power of Introverts in a World that Can't Stop Talking* (2012) by Susan Cain, make the case to simply leave us introverts alone. We do not want to mingle, accept an award or watch people accept awards, and we do not want to sit idly and absorb the idiocy that radiates from meetings.

Once a recognition of that experience connects with introverted people; the point could be made that introverts are, historically oppressed by an extroverted society. Can we doubt that introverted people, who do not engage in any social-media aggrandizing or office leg-humping fail to get promoted like extroverted people? What rectifies this situation? Should we have an "introvert awareness" day? Or, should we celebrate introverted people with an Introvert Month? (This might create a public argument over who counts as an introvert, which would be about as useful as analyzing the shade of someone's skin tone for its shade of blackness.)

The problem with historical grievances is that if the past did not occur precisely in the way in which it did, then none of us would exist. Take the question, "Is it good that slavery existed?" The answer, for everyone currently alive, must be "yes," or none of us would be here. If we posit that existence is better than nonexistence, a bias we are mostly forced into since the nonexistent have no voice, then it is good that everything that happened in the past actually happened. Some philosophers would dismiss this case as "presentism" and reject the notion that existence is better than nonexistence, and that's just a fundamental disagreement that cannot be altered.

This logic makes any attempt to connect present conditions to historical wrongs difficult. If the purpose of recognizing historical wrongs is to understand the development of a present state, this can be useful, but if it is to develop a sense of historical identity, then it becomes problematic. For example, in 1860, the United States harbored about four million slaves. That is roughly the population of modern Oklahoma. The entirety of the trans-Atlantic slave trade included about 12.5 million slaves who were captured from West Africa (by West Africans) and taken across the Atlantic by European and American slave traders.

The experience of being a slave belongs only to the slaves; it's not a hereditary grievance. Likewise, the experience of being a slaveholder is an experience that belongs only to slaveholders. Privilege and poverty are generational, but those of us in the present cannot necessarily correct for those past wrongs. How can 325 million Americans, and seven billion people on the planet, be beholden to a past connected to populations that are historically rather small?

We might all think of ourselves as Citizens of the Present, and we must decide, in the present, how much identity should be developed around our immutable characteristics. This brings up hard questions: is deafness a disability or an identity? If it is an identity, and the deaf have legions who believe that deafness is a culture of its own worth celebrating, then to "cure" deafness is to eliminate a vibrant culture. Should Citizens of the Present try to cure disabilities or create an environment that is welcoming to people from all different backgrounds?

That becomes the better goal for diversity because without it, organizations become trapped in systems of implicit bias. Imagine a middle-aged male who is asked to create a jogging track. He might enjoy running out into the country and might always feel safe in doing so because male runners are rarely or never harassed. Yet a 2019 *Runner's Weekly* survey found that 85% of female runners experience harassment and feel unsafe; if they had input into how to create a walking/jogging track they might make it circular and contain it within a well-lit space. This is what makes diversity valuable.

In a strange way, questions about identity actually connect with sentimentality. We might ask what it means to be sentimental about an object. Say that a child has a stuffed animal that helped her emotionally during her cancer treatments as a toddler. Later, that stuffed animal is lost. Should the parents replace the stuffed animal that looked just like the lost one?

The answer depends upon how sophisticated the child's awareness is. If the child will know the difference between the "real" stuffed animal and the new one, then trying to pass off a replacement would likely cause a wailing fit.

Why? Before the child received it, the stuffed animal was just one of millions that had been coldly manufactured. However, when the child grasped the animal during a long process of cancer treatment, she connected a feeling of comfort, chemically encoded into a neurological pattern, that only the "real" stuffed animal could trigger.

Something similar occurs among collectors. A book collector, for example, is not really collecting books, but collecting the feeling of comfort that comes while sitting in a library. The same is true for art collection or, probably, just about any kind of collecting. If someone gets a little shot of dopamine from knowing that he owns a rare copy of the First Folio of Shakespeare, then the knowledge that the First Folio was actually a third edition could create a new neurological pathway that ruins the emotional experience and maybe even replaces that positive experience with a negative one.

How interesting is that? Someone could be feeling perfectly content with a book in her collector's library one moment, but a second after finding out that the same book is a "fake," she could be irate at having been duped. This phenomenon is very similar to what child psychologists call Fear of Missing Out (FOMO), which is especially prevalent among teen and tween children. An 11-year-old girl can be happily playing by herself in the backyard until she gets a message somehow that all of her friends are at a birthday party that she was not invited to. How can that simple piece of knowledge, which in no practical way is interfering with the play she was previously enjoying, ruing this girl's mood?

Similarly, a woman who identifies as African-American might be distraught over the discovery that the majority of her genes are Irish, or that she is descended from Jamaicans rather than from African-American slaves. A man who identified with a Prussian ancestry might suddenly be distraught by discovering that his great-grandparents were in fact from Russia. These little snippets of knowledge can interrupt previously established chemical and neurological patterns and in this way disrupt a sense of identity.

When identity is created around activities, the problem can be more significant. There is a difference between someone who says "My name is Kate and I teach," and someone who says "My name is Kate and I am a teacher." Or, "My name is Josh and I skate" versus "My name is Josh and I am a skater." The first sentences in both cases make a distinction between a sovereign person with an identity and the activity. The second statement blends the two.

So there is a difference between saying "My name is Kate and I lack the ability to hear" and "My name is Kate and I am deaf." Or, "My name is Denise and I have black skin" and "My name is Denise and I am African-American." When Kate calls herself deaf she is identifying with a community, and deafness is a trait connected to her sense of herself. The same is true when Denise calls herself African-American. In the case of Denise, she would be connecting her identity to a historical identity and a collective experience. Is Kate doing the same thing? If so, then finding medical "cures" for deafness could amount to eliminating a community.

But what about Autism or Down's Syndrome? Is it "Hi my name is Howard and I have autism," or "My name is Howard and I am autistic?" Is there a separate person from the autism, or are the two syncretized entirely? It would seem that the two are syncretized; that certainly must be true for Down's Syndrome. A person with Down's was never anything but a person with Down's. Yet, Down's Syndrome is still treated as a disorder afflicting a "normal" baby. Women who are pregnant or seeking to become pregnant can find a variety of behaviors, including drug or alcohol use, that might put the fetus "at risk" of being born with Down's Syndrome. One of those behaviors is conceiving the child too late in life.

This brings up a series of questions, the first of which is, "Is Down's an identity, and if so, then what is wrong with engaging in behaviors that make it more likely a child will be born with Down's?" A pregnant woman who drank and consumed illegal narcotics might face some moral condemnation for giving birth to a child with Down's because the thinking is that a "normal" child was on its way but that the mother's behavior created this change. A variety of cognitive defects in children can be traced to the mother's behavior while pregnant.

However, a woman who chose to conceive a child later in life and then gave birth to a Down's baby would be unlikely to face any "blame." In 2008, Sarah Palin, the then-governor of Alaska, ran on John McCain's ticket and proudly mentioned that she had a son with Down's. Palin had given birth at an advanced age, which statistically makes the birth of a child with Down's more likely. Yet, Palin suffered from no public moral condemnation (nor should she have), likely because aging is not seen by the public as a risky behavior. However, having a child at an advanced age is just as much a choice as choosing to drink heavily while pregnant, so that brings up questions about whether Down's is an identity or a "syndrome."

Of course, people who identify as African-American, or with deaf culture, etc., could claim that their sense of identity has been shaped for them by exclusionist laws and cultures. Granted, but the problem with such an identity is that when the restrictive laws and cultures loosen then the core identity can become threatened. If preservation of that identity becomes a necessity, then something like a "micro-aggression" can be deemed the equivalent of Jim Crow laws. This is also an issue with cancer patients; sometimes after years of treatment, it can be traumatic for a cancer patient to learn that she is in remission.

At some level, identity must be a neurological state that can be interrupted by changes in information. This must also be the connection between people and the objects they are sentimental about; if a beloved object puts a person into a pleasant neurological state, and if the knowledge that another similar object is not the "real" thing alters that pleasant experience, then that is what it is. If our language encodes activities and immutable characteristics, rather than the development of ethics, relationships, or talents that are of some service to society, then these identity questions will continue to cause confusion.

Students should be familiar with discussions about race and identity, given that the subject buzzes constantly in the background at all times and often becomes the focal point of discussion in public and classroom settings. As is apparent, however, from the examples used in this chapter, the subject of identity is rarely thought about with any depth of understanding. It's as if questions of identity put up a force field that rejects any attempt at philosophical inquiry, but philosophical inquiry should never be rejected on the premise that it threatens assumptions.

KEY IDEAS

- The concept of identity and its connection with the historical past often creates fallacious forms of reasoning. The people of the present only exist because everything in the past occurred precisely as it did. To create ethical judgements about the past too often creates the hypothetical and fallacious idea that the past could be altered to a better present that includes everyone currently alive.
- The impact of identity on a creative work can be examined by imagining the "true" author to be of a different race or ethnicity than he or she really is.
- "Identity" itself might be considered a manufactured creation; one might be able to imagine a variety of manufactured identities that could be created and connected to a modern experience.
- Language encodes certain thought processes about identity, so that "Karen is a nice person who likes to skateboard" is a fundamentally different statement that "Karen is a skateboarder."
- The connection between a person and his or her identity is really a connection between a persona and a certain neurological state, something similar to how people react to sentimental objects or collector's items.

Chapter Seven

Ethics

Intellectuals like the notion of using a small number of principles to describe a large number of phenomena. Isaac Newton managed to describe the workings of the macro-universe using just three postulates: 1. What goes up must come down. 2. Every action has an equal and opposite reaction. 3. Objects in motion will stay in motion unless acted upon by an outside force. Sarcastic philosophers of epistemology can always mess with physicists with questions like "can you define '"down?"'" (answer: whichever way gravity is pulling the hardest—the lunar rover came "down" on the moon), but the descriptive power of Newton's natural philosophy is overwhelmingly impressive. Charles Darwin needed just two concepts, natural and sexual selection, to describe the panorama and phantasmagoria of the natural world. Can something similar be done with ethics?

No. No. No. No simple set of postulates exists which can guide ethical behavior. The two most popular ethical postulates, the Golden Rule and Kant's Categorical Imperative, cannot meet the challenge of thought experiments and quickly dissolve into uselessness when confronted with basic thought experiments. Here's how.

THE GOLDEN RULE: DO UNTO OTHERS AS YOU WOULD HAVE OTHERS DO UNTO YOU

Even liberal minded Christians, including those who don't see the Bible as literal history and truth, consider the Golden Rule (partially espoused by the literary character of Jesus) as being a durable bit of ancient wisdom. But how well does it survive a philosophical examination?

Consider a sexual predator in a position of power, say, a Hollywood producer, who makes advances on a woman. He is doing to her what he would have her do unto him, isn't he? This could hardly be called ethical. At this point, your mind is probably protesting that I am mischaracterizing the Golden Rule and that the real point of it is to generally treat people with respect. After all, if the Hollywood producer was in a vulnerable position, would he want to be advanced upon by a person in power?

How do we know that this is not the case? Sadists and masochists and sado-masochists are everywhere, and they might perfectly well like having their rights violated by someone in power and, based on that, would feel perfectly justified in doing this to someone else. You can see the immediate problem with the Golden Rule: it's subjective to the individual's sense of ethics, not a universal dictum.

A judge, for example, might release a murderer under the dictum of, "If I was in his position, I would like to be released without punishment." But this would upset the family of the victim, so the judge should put the murderer away for life because "if I was the victim's family, that's what I would have done unto me." Ethical issues affect people across a spectrum, and decisions often have to be made that affect multiple individuals in ways that may be opposed to one another. How, then, can this simplistic ethical dictum be applied?

Kant's Categorical Imperative

Immanuel Kant (1724–1804) developed a wordy philosophy around the notion that every ethical action should be judged by subjecting it to the question of (in paraphrase), "What if my action were to become a universal dictum for behavior?" If you are doing something, goes the logic, imagine what would happen if everyone else did the same thing? If that would have a positive outcome then the action is likely ethical. If it would have a negative outcome, then it likely is not ethical.

For example, if you picked up trash by the highway, this would seem to be ethical, because if everyone acted in that same way, then all of the trash would get picked up. Great, right? Well, now. If everyone stopped to pick up trash then other work would not get done, people would be in danger of getting hit by cars, and altruistic individuals would glut the ditches by the highway. Some people, like the elderly or those undergoing chemotherapy, might get sick in the heat, etc.

There's also a "trench warfare" challenge to the categorical imperative (mentioned in an earlier chapter), where we could imagine 10 soldiers from Country A in one trench and 10 soldiers from Country B in another trench.

If a soldier from Country A refuses to fight, he could justify that action by stating, "Well, if everyone stops fighting then we all survive," but if no one else follows his dictum, then he has merely committed suicide and helped his comrades to get killed.

The categorical imperative therefore runs into two serious problems: 1. A "universal" application of one's own moral rules assumes that others have the same background as the person making the ethical decision. This is another reason why the mythology of Jesus gives very little real moral guidance; when Jesus comes across the sick, he can heal them, a superpower not available to mortals. 2. The extent of the "universal" application of morality is not clear. Does that extend to the other side of the trench, or just to a specific group? If we change the question of "what if everyone did what I am doing" to "what if everyone in my group (however defined) did what I am doing?" then a trench soldier should fire back, not lay down arms.

No single principle or set of principles can be applied to ethical cases because the situations and circumstances can alter outcomes so much. This means that ethical reasoning is dependent upon something that logicians, and certainly mathematicians, are much less comfortable with: analogy-making.

Consider the old ethical conversation-maker of abortion. Religious disagreement really does not cause the topic of abortion to be controversial; abortion's controversy comes from the ambivalent status of a pregnant women concerning natural rights theory. Natural rights theory treats each individual as a person with rights that are to be respected; each person can exercise a right until doing so interferes with someone else's rights.

This works fine for sovereign individuals of sound mind, such as when two people over eighteen years of age enter into a contract, and it works well when the harm one party does is obvious, such as when second-hand smoke floats over into the lungs of non-smokers. However, natural rights theory cannot deal well at all with a combination of human beings, which is what a pregnant woman is.

For people who want a simplistic ethics involving abortion, there are two options. Either A. life begins at conception, which means imparting the status of "human" onto a newly fertilized blastocyst, or B. life begins after a fetus slides out of the birth canal and into the open air, which means that a movement of just a few inches actually determines a person's legal status. Either of these positions could be considered logically absurd, but that's what often happens when an analogical argument is examined at either extreme and the ends are compared to each other.

It would be just as absurd to state that a picture of a newly born baby and the actual person of a 90-year-old man are the same being. The 90-year-old man has likely changed cells entirely 18 times since his time as a baby and the only direct genetic connection between the two would come in the form of a set of genetic predispositions. The daily changeover of cells, where the person on Tuesday is closely analogous to the person on Monday or Wednesday, is what causes the sense of continuity.

Despite being the most practical branch of philosophy, ethics rarely gets taught in a formal way at any level of education. This is likely because the subject tends not to fit within ordinary logical constraints in the same way that math or even computer programming do. "Ordinary" logic as defined by philosophers tends to operate under binary conditions, such as if A is true then B must be true.

Most literate people are familiar with the basic syllogistic structure of formal Aristotelian logic, and it's usually explained like this:

A. All philosophers are men. B. Socrates is a man. C. Therefore, Socrates is a philosopher.

Anyone can immediately pick up on three points here. A. This logic is false; just because all philosophers are men that does not mean that all men are philosophers. B. The false reasoning led to the right conclusion in this case, which might cause a further categorization error at a later point. C. The first statement is disputable, as philosophers are not always men.

The Greeks also developed early mathematics, and so logic and math became intertwined, which led to the creation of "truth tables" that indicate all of the combinations of truth and falsehood that can arise between two statements.

For example: A and B can either both be true (T,T), A can be true and B false (T,F), A can be false and B true (F,T) or both can be false (F,F). Truth tables operate like binary code in the sense that an information receptacle can either be turned on or off (1 or 0) but has no room for ambiguity or change.

It's important to remember that, despite its importance for the computer industry, binary code was developed in the 17th century by Newton's German rival Gottfried Wilhelm Leibniz (1646–1716) as an alternative to the use of Arabic numerals. Binary code can only be used in conjunction with extraordinary memory, which is why it lay tucked away on history's intellectual shelf until computer programmers, with their newly developed transistors, pulled it down in the middle of the 20th Century.

But binary logical analysis and truth tables operate only under certain self-contained conditions; one must assume the premise or (A) statement to be true in order for the process to work. For abortion ethics, a truth table would look like this:

A. A fetus is a life. B. A fetus is not a life.

We now have only two options on the truth table A. (T) and B. (F), or A (F) and B. (T). These both cannot be true and they both cannot be false.

Again, reasoning from a premise creates a logical structure of its own, regardless of the truth of the premise statement. Unfortunately, logical statements are as subject to statistical whims as any other type of statement, and sometimes faulty logic leads to a true conclusion. For example:

A. Prayer heals people. B. I prayed for my sick friend. C. My sick friend was healed.

Obviously, a certain percentage of sick people are going to get better no matter what, and the prayer would have to be isolated and parceled out for statistical significance, but that would not necessarily be a problem in a logical sequence. Let's try one more.

A. God is good. B. Horrible things happen. If A is true then B must be false. If B is true then A must be false.

There is an assumption here that "God" contains "omnipotent" as a character trait. One could conclude that A. God is good and B. horrible things happen by positing that God is less than all powerful, but that logical chain is as meaningless as A. Grandma is good and B. horrible things happen. Logic, therefore, tends to deal only with "whole number" solutions.

Consider this lengthy but necessary passage from Morris Kline's classic *Mathematics for the Nonmathematician* (1967):

Historically, one of the motivations for the study of the algebra of sets was provided by the study of logic. Mathematicians, notably Descartes and Leibniz, were so much impressed by the usefulness of ordinary algebra that they conceived the idea of inventing an algebra for reasoning in all fields of thought. The concepts of ethics, politics, economics, and philosophy would be the analogues of numbers, and the relationships among these concepts would be the analogues of the operations of arithmetic. They referred to this plan as universal algebra. The work of Descartes and Leibniz was not successful because they undertook too much. . . . However, about 1850, George Boole, one of the founders of mathematical logic, showed that the reasoning processes themselves, which are

studied in logic, can be formalized and carried out by an algebra of logic which
is identical with the algebra of sets (p. 495).

Boole's genius is secured in mathematical history, but by connecting logic
to algebra, he calcified the process and made it all but inapplicable to ethics.
Had Boole connected logic to calculus, which allows for fluidity in movement, then ethics would have a system of thought that moves like a snake
rather than like a giraffe.

Unlike algebra, calculus contains the notion of the derivative which allows for changes to the nth degree between numbers (nth meaning whatever
number can be plugged in.) There are about fourteen major rules for dif-
ferentiation in calculus but let's focus on just one, the General Leibniz rule.
This gives two points F and G, and states that there can be nth numbers of
difference between them.

So, rather than developing a system of if A is true then B is true, the truth
could be connected to the nth degree. Truth would operate more as an alge-
braic function where if the initial statement (X) changes, then that alters the
position of the affected (Y) statement. We could alter our ethics as the situation changes and this would be more applicable to cases of ethics. Unlike
in algebra, however, the function would operate in two directions so that a
change in Y would affect a change in X.

For example, consider these abortion scenarios:

(X) A woman is four months pregnant. (Y) Her husband leaves her and she
loses her job.
(X) A woman is four months pregnant. (Y) She is concerned about how a
baby will change the free lifestyle that she and her husband enjoy.
(X) A woman is nine months pregnant. (Y) Her husband leaves her and she
loses her job.
(X) A woman is nine months pregnant. (Y) Her husband stays with her but
both lose their jobs.

When the X stays the same but the Y changes, then the ethics might shift.
In calculus, objects sometimes move fast, and so can situational ethics. We
could imagine the ethical calculus needed in a hospital situation where a baby
is about to be born but the mother's health is at tremendous risk because of
this.

Please remember that this ethical calculus is not intended to be an argument for legal change. The case is often made that legal restrictions on abortion merely drive the practice underground, where, as an illegal activity, it

becomes more dangerous. The point here is merely to state that the ethical practice of abortion can be addressed with a fluid form of ethics (and yes, this form of thinking leads to a pro-choice position, since outlawing all abortion does not allow for a fluidity of ethical thought.)

Although this might sound strange, or even a little like "measuring poetry" from the famous *Dead Poets Society* (1989) scene where Mr. Keating (Robin Williams) eventually tells his students to start ripping out pages of their English textbook, it is possible to put numbers on ethics. Let's imagine a fetus with a "life score" of between one and one hundred. There are roughly 270 days in a pregnancy, which means the life score of the fetus would go up 1 point every 2.7 days.

If the X has 270 points, then the Y should have 275, because the mother is a fully formed being and in control of the decision. This does not always mean that Y will determine X ethically, but it will keep the balance of ethics toward the health of the mother.

After 3 months the fetus would have a life score of 33.33. If we plug that into the X we get 33.33 (X). What's the score of the crisis that might cause a woman to terminate pregnancy?

Loss of job = 25, Health crisis that might affect pregnancy = 275.

X=33.33, Y=25.

This ethical balance would lead toward carrying the baby, but a X=33.33 and a Y=275 would point toward abortion. The further along in the pregnancy a fetus is, the heavier the Y will have to be.

We might consider rape or incest in this situation. A 13-year-old girl who is pregnant from rape would be a 275, which would give the Y number the ethical strength in the equation over the X in every case. This would make it ethical to terminate a pregnancy even in the ninth month if a girl was pregnant from rape. However, the difference between Y and X might only be five. In the case of smaller numerical differences; there would be leeway for discussion in the way that there might not be if the difference was larger.

A pregnant 13-year-old who is three days pregnant would have a difference between Y and X of over 272 points. That overwhelmingly points to the ethics of aborting in that case. However, in the 9th month, it might be possible that a young girl could undergo worse trauma from the abortion than from the birth and, with a difference of only five, that would allow for decision-making from those closest to the decision-making.

If this causes you to recoil, then consider the alternative, which is to offer no ethical guidance at all in these difficult cases, to abandon reason entirely, and to base decisions on gut decisions that ethically divide people into (frequently) binary decision-making processes. An ethical calculus will guide decision-making in difficult situations and lead to a greater level on ethical consensus.

Since it defies traditional logical structures; ethics can only be approached analogically. The process of analogical thinking lends itself to a particular kind of dialogue, where individuals can work through a discussion to come to a conclusion. (Incidentally, based on this, the National High School Ethics Bowl and the National Collegiate Ethics Bowl focus on teaching "competitors" how to dialogue rather than debate).

Another application of ethical calculus is to ask: how does reasoning by analogy for ethics work? We must begin with extremes, at a point where universal (or almost universal) agreement exists, and then bring the situations inward concentrically from each other. For example, we might ask the question of "What does the Second Amendment protect?" The term "arms," referring to what Americans have a right to bear, is rather ambiguous.

Start with an extreme case where just about any reasonable person would agree and then, concentrically develop less extreme cases until the agreement dissipates. For example, should the Second Amendment cover an individual's right to own a hydrogen bomb? If two people agree that, no, an individual should not own a hydrogen bomb, then what about an atom bomb, or stealth bomber, or a tank? If one person says no to a stealth bomber but yes to a tank, then it's incumbent upon that person to explain why a tank and a stealth bomber are different.

The discovery of disagreement is not cause for argument, but for dialogue. Dialogue can lead to greater levels of truth and was seen by the Greeks as being intrinsic to philosophy.

Let's apply this ethical calculus to some "work" problems in ethics and see what kind of answers arise. Some of these cases are built from real-world cases, and some have even appeared in the National High School Ethics Bowl, but they are made generic and hypothetical for the purposes here.

Case #1: Two Deaf Parents Want Doctors to Ensure that Their Child Will be Deaf by Instituting an In-Utero Procedure

Is deafness a disability or an identity? If one defines deafness as a disability, then the deliberate creation of a disability in a child is clearly unethical. But deaf people tend not to define themselves as disabled, especially when schools for the deaf seem to have created a culture of deafness that is all its own. That culture is as well defined as any other and has characteristics such as constant social contact, bluntness, and a strong sense of community. Nothing is wrong with deaf people, so what is wrong with creating more deaf people?

Using an ethical calculus, set X as a moral absolute where deafness is 100% a disability and Y as a moral absolute where deafness is an 100% identity. For ease, let's assign a score of one hundred to each.

Now, set up similarity and difference tables and look for an analogy.

Deafness and Identity, Similarities

1. Language
2. Intra-group status
3. Special schools
4. Group gatherings
5. High rates of intermarriage

Deafness and Identity, Differences

1. Deafness makes connecting to the hearing world more difficult than ordinary identities
2. Deafness has varying degrees
3. Many deaf people seek "corrective" processes so they can hear
4. Many deaf people are born to "hearing" parents

From this, it's actually possible to state that deafness might be 60% an identity, which would give it a score of 60. How much of deafness is a disability?

Deafness and Disability, Similarities

1. Makes integration to the standard, hearing world, difficult
2. Deaf children are often born to hearing parents, which makes family integration more difficult
3. Deaf people require special help to integrate with the standard, hearing world in the same way that people in wheelchairs need ramps, or blind people need dogs
4. Deaf people, like most disabled people, can make contributions to society
5. Deafness is not always a born condition; it can be caused by an accident or a slow moving condition

Deafness and Disability, Differences

1. Deafness need not be a permanent condition
2. Deafness contains a culture and language of its own in a way that not even
   people in wheelchairs, for example, have developed

Now, weight these and note that the key difference between Deafness as an
Identity and Deafness as a Disability is that deafness need not be a permanent
condition. It is possible to temporarily create deafness by, say, wearing dense
headphones. If that sounds ridiculous, why?

Hearing-impaired children who go to schools where "hearing" is the norm
routinely wear hearing aids or cochlear implants. Why could it not be the case
where a child with "normal" hearing would wear dense headphones in order
to attend a deaf school? If deafness is 100% a culture, then cultures are open
to people who are outside of that norm. A hearing child of deaf parents could
be as bilingual in culture and language as an American-born child of Mexican
parents. If a procedure was available to prevent a child from learning English,
that would likely be considered unethical as well.

Case #2: Mixed Martial Arts and Consent

Mixed Martial Arts (MMA) does not usually become the center of philosophical discussion, but MMA provides an interesting problem of consent. MMA
fighters routinely get hit several times in fights even after they are concussed
and are lying supine on the ground. This brings up a question: does being
knocked out remove the consent of the fighter, making any subsequent blows
landed by the conscious fighter (presumably the winner) illegal?

Can a conscious person consent to having harm done to him while he is
unconscious? Almost certainly not—the only analogous case we have where
a conscious person consents to something happening to her while she's
unconscious is in surgery. Surgeries are supposed to help people, not harm
them, so there is no real precedent for someone consenting to be harmed
while lacking consciousness.

The ethical calculus here might take the form of a risk/reward assessment.
If the X is the reward, which is presumably why the fighter is taking the risk,
then the Y is the risk. To be clear, the Y is not the risk of losing the fight, as
precedent makes it fairly clear that people can consent to engage in all sorts
of dangerous things. The risk is of being hit once or more while unconscious,
which is hard to justify ethically.

Again, let's assign the X a value of one hundred and the Y a value of one hundred and then bring them together. What reward is worth the risk of being beaten while unconscious? An X of one hundred would likely have to be balanced against a Y of one for the ratio to come into focus. This might make the risk/reward come into focus for individual fighters, but even then, if they consent to a fight while conscious, it's not clear they can legally or ethically consent to being harmed while unconscious.

At this point, we must assess the ability of MMA organizations to actually prevent a fighter from being pummeled after unconsciousness. Technically, this should not occur, as the referee should stop the fight at the moment someone cannot continue. In practice, fighters are repeatedly hit numerous times after unconsciousness because the referee cannot step in fast enough. Should MMA organizers be allowed to create an arena of possibility where someone can be pummeled after being knocked unconscious?

That question is interesting because one would have to balance X as the positive good that MMA does for society versus Y, the risk it poses to individuals who might be rendered unconscious and then beaten afterward. It's hard to justify the existence of MMA under those terms, so it really should not exist at all.

Case #3: Cosmetic Surgery

A mother who took her daughter in, at age 10 or 11, for a nose job done for cosmetic reasons, might be accused of abuse. However, a mother who takes her daughter in to have metal vices put on her child's teeth, which are then tightened at regular intervals in a painful process designed to restructure the development of the girl's teeth, would be considered normal. Why are braces considered to be an acceptable cosmetic procedure for children, where other forms of cosmetic procedures would be considered abusive?

Developing an ethical calculus is not necessary here, as the reader can feel free to treat this as a "work problem." The concept is presented for the purpose of developing the ability to think about the analogy. Clearly, a nose job is more invasive than braces, and any time an anesthetic is involved it increases the risk to the patient substantially. Yet a nose job to correct a breathing problem would probably be considered acceptable for someone at any age, and if a more aesthetically pleasing nose was shaped in the process of correcting the underlying breathing problem, few would blanch at that.

Braces are often justified for kids because they help to "correct" problems like an overbite, and orthodontists will point out any number of minor mouth problems that might develop in children who don't get braces. Yet braces can't be all that essential because Medicaid only covers braces in children if the braces are deemed "medically necessary." In most cases, braces are put on kids as an elective treatment to correct minor problems and to develop a nice smile.

Essentially, then, braces can be considered a cosmetic procedure that are performed on children at the behest of their parents. Ultimately, the straight smile indicates something about a person's background. A 20-year-old university student with straight teeth can signal to others that she comes from at least a middle-class background and that she had people in her life who cared enough about her to take her to an orthodontist. Straight teeth are undoubtedly better than crooked teeth for a variety of reasons, but the primary effect, in most cases, of braces is to create a cosmetic change.

Given this, do we need to rethink cosmetic procedures as a whole? What, exactly, is wrong with face-lifts, fat freezing, or breast implants? The media gleefully reports any minor uptick in cancer rates that come from something like breast implants, but they don't report the positive changes in mood or outlook that might come from a cosmetic procedure. How dangerous does a cosmetic procedure have to be before it's unethical, and why do we act like cosmetic procedures are only done out of selfishness or narcissism?

Just about anyone who thinks about the problems inherent to philosophy realizes that emotions tend to hinder the process of logical thinking. We are sort of comfortable with this idea when we consider anger or prejudice as emotions, but the notion that empathy or love for others can cause harmmakes people less comfortable. Situations routinely arise in ethics, where one needs to make an ethical decision that could harm one person or group but be beneficial to others.

The notion that we should act ethically in a way that benefits groups, developed first by Jeremy Bentham and then further by his student John Stuart Mill, is too often dismissed and more often misunderstood. The greatest good for the greatest number can never involve the infringement upon individual rights because creating moral conditions in which it is okay to, for example, imprison someone without due process, ends up creating a negative effect on everyone. If something could be done to your neighbor, it could be done to you, and the insecurity that comes from knowing that does damage to the greater good.

Still, Universalism as a philosophy can only help as a general guide, usually to public policy, and it usually does not help with the development of individual principles. This was made clear in the 2020 COVID-19 pandemic, when governments tried to encourage people to stay inside and stay home, but young men and women in the United States and the world could not (or chose not to) cognitively connect their decisions to party on a Florida beach, or hang out in a Florentine café, with the deaths of older people with underlying health issues.

This is not to necessarily shame younger people who wanted to carry on with their 2020 spring breaks. They are caught in what might be called the "take your place" dilemma. For example, an environmentalist might want to fight carbon emissions by not flying on a plane, but whether her seat is filled or not, the plane will take off and fly. Therefore, she will have inconvenienced herself and done no good for the environment at all. Why not remove the inconvenience to the self in such a case?

That kind of question paralyzes any approach to solving any large-scale problem. If someone is entertained by high school football, but concerned about the impact of concussions on children, then one could conclude that since other people are watching the high school football game, and the game is going to go on not matter what, why not attend?

The end result of such thinking is that individuals fall back on the "if you don't want your kid to play football, then don't let them play, but my son is playing" argument regarding personal choice. But personal choice, especially regarding children in a family, clearly has limits, so why does football exist at all?

This is one of the reasons that a divide forms between liberals and conservatives over these issues, with liberals preferring large-scale legislation to reduce choices that may cause harm, and conservatives defending those choices as necessary individual freedoms. A political system defined by individual liberties really cannot adjust to ethics that require a mass response. War, of a certain kind, seems to be the only thing that can galvanize a sense of shared sacrifice and even that has its limits.

Why would a 20-year-old stay home from a party when someone would take his place and the coronavirus would continue to spread nonetheless? Why inconvenience oneself while in the process doing no good to the cause? Governors and mayors soon found that to try and rely upon the public's desire to act, of their own volition, for the greater good was to do no good at all. Authoritarian measures had to be invoked in order to get people to stay home.

Interestingly, this type of ethical problem connects with Isaac Asimov's (1920–1992) famous principles for Artificial Intelligence in his famous book *I, Robot* (1950).

- A robot may not injure a human being or, through inaction, allow a human being to come to harm.

- A robot must obey orders given it by human beings except where such orders would conflict with the First Law.
- A robot must protect its own existence as long as such protection does not conflict with the First or Second Law.

The fun of reading *I, Robot* comes from watching Asimov develop clever ethical scenarios that will challenge these three principles. Still, how could the all-important "First Law" deal with a Rube Goldberg contraption where someone put a marble on a track that then triggered a series of events that led, say, to a boot kicking some old lady in the rear? Would the robot be able to connect the dropping of the marble to the movement of the boot, or would the marble only be connected directly to the next action?

If we had police robots programmed with these principles, how would they have reacted to the COVID-19 outbreak? If they had acted on forcing people to stay home, they could have caused harm to those individuals, but if they allowed healthy people to go to restaurants and bars, that might have caused harm to others via inaction. What if the ability to help is beyond the capacity of any individual robot? To go back to our trench warfare scenario, a robot might only be capable of stopping one side from firing. To do so would protect the people on the other side but harm the people in the trench that the robot can control.

Likewise, people who are unlikely to be harmed by something like coronavirus themselves, but could potentially carry the virus to vulnerable populations, might find it difficult to directly connect their actions to harming others. Who can blame the kids, though? The data regarding COVID-19 quickly began to look reminiscent of the nutritional advice given out by whatever organizations research these things; we could not tell just how deadly the virus was because the number of people infected was undetectable. People only showed up to be tested when symptoms drove them to the doctor.

But the media spectacle around the coronavirus sent people with a mild headache and chills, or people with the sniffles, to the doctors in droves. Broad testing sent the numbers of infected soaring even as deaths attributed to the virus in certain areas of the world continued to rise. Italy suffered the most, as about 8% of those diagnosed with COVID-19 died from it. Armchair mathematicians posted that number on various population centers and assured us that a modern plague had descended upon humanity and that the only acceptable immediate action involved shutting down population centers.

No one could create a cost-benefit analysis on the situation; how much economic damage could a nation endure to save a few years for the elderly (the average age of death in Italy neared 80)? How much damage could the virus actually do? The numbers in Germany and South Korea appeared vastly more optimistic than in China, Iran, or Italy; why was this? What underlying conditions created the worst scenarios? Should Minneapolis react with a total shutdown of meeting places, or could they expect a more benign scenario like what Berlin or Seoul experienced?

Western civilization, when confronted with large scale ethical questions, simply crashed. Everything shut down; the notion that it might be best to quarantine vulnerable populations while everyone else continued working got shouted down by the advice of medical professionals who worried that every hospital in Europe or the United States might soon become overwhelmed like those in a few Italian provinces. The Center for Disease Control (CDC), with exponential algorithms in their eyes, shouted advice at government officials who probably had not had a math class since junior high school.

No one could really articulate why the dining room of a McDonalds in Grant County, Indiana needed to shut down because 78-year-old smokers were dying in Italy. No one could question underlying assumptions about populations and their propensity to succumb to the virus. It was hard to point out that people die every day, and that some of the deaths associated to coronavirus might have been due more to age and underlying conditions than to the virus itself.

How could we weigh the cost of a million single mothers, suddenly deprived of service jobs, against the deaths spread by the virus? No one could point out that such a balance might be a false dilemma, that the schools and restaurants could stay open if the vulnerable populations could be shielded. The problem was framed as binary: Lives or the Economy, when the choice really was between hospitals being overloaded with a functioning economy or hospitals being overloaded without a functioning economy.

Rationalists realized that the world is not rational—people in distress seek constant information, and soon fake cures spread; people took toxins in hopes that it would act as a prophylactic against the virus. The stock market dropped, schools closed for "e-learning" options, and everyone seemed to forget that government money came from taxing the private sector. Millions of people jumped off the working person's treadmill and on to the social safety net at the same time.

Did people realize that everything that had once been thought important wasn't? Sports got shut down and no one really needed a college coach or an NBA team. Sanitation workers, teachers, grocery store clerks, and nurses looked heroic. No one needed any of the worthless bureaucrats that choke society with their absurdities. The SATs, ACTs, and umpteen other school tests got dropped or modified in the crisis, prompting the question of if these could be eliminated so quickly, then how important were they in the first place?

It was never clear why everyone was supposed to stay home, except for going to the grocery store, gas station, or to essential jobs. How did that help? Grocery stores and gas stations would simply become focal points of transmission. If COVID-19 was that contagious, just shutting down gathering places would not necessarily be effective in slowing the transmission, not if people all funneled to grocery stores. Then, when people bought a bunch of groceries all at once so that they could stay home for a prolonged period of time, they were castigated for "panic buying" and stressing the grocery supply chain.

COVID-19 became the worst kind of problem: a natural disaster that gave bureaucrats the illusion of control and, therefore, public culpability for a failure to act. Nonsensical emergency measures, based off of incomplete data, went into place across Western civilization. The de facto message that the lives of gas station clerks, waitresses and waiters handling takeout orders, grocery store workers, and Amazon employees really mattered less than everyone else became clear.

How do we connect actions to the public good without reliable data about the impact of those actions?

Ethics Applied to World History

It is always statistically tricky to determine what the cause of an effect is. So, in some way, is it fair to say that loose gun control laws are a causal factor in a certain amount of suicides? Statistically speaking, loose gun laws are connected to suicide rates simply because suicidal people can get easy access to a gun. Could it be stated, then, that communism led to the COVID-19 global pandemic? Yes it can, and history offers some interesting lessons for correction of that cause. However, people living in liberal democracies must stop focusing on the speck on their own eyes, and see the beam sticking out of communism's eye.

Citizens of the world who lived through 2020 might have been thinking that *this* is what history looks like. COVID-19 infects human beings of every nationality and spreads from person to person in the slums of Delhi, the crowded prisons of Mexico City, through the mosques of Pakistan and Iran, and into the grocery stores and assisted living centers of the United States. Fear of viral infection has effectively shut down society and halted international financial markets. What caused the viral outbreak? An epidemiologist might declare that the "wet markets" of Wuhan, China created a biological environment that allowed for the evolution of COVID-19. Saying that, however, is like saying that meltdown of a nuclear reaction on April 26, 1986, in Soviet-controlled Ukraine was due to faulty engineering. The cause of COVID-19, like the cause of the Chernobyl meltdown, is ultimately communist ideology and the pairing of rapid economic and military growth pushed by a government that is unchecked by the will of a free people. The virus spread in a Western civilization that was unprepared for it, but it is important for us in the West to understand that the virus had a political as well as biological cause. Below are three historical causes of the COVID-19 epidemic, and recommendation for a political cure.

The Communist Party in China thrives on a memory of historical humiliation. Modern Americans cannot understand what it is like to have our political system directed by outsiders, but our country as a political entity has existed for less than 250 years. Chinese civilization goes back over three thousand years and, for most of that, Chinese considered themselves to be the "Middle Kingdom," a phrase that indicated their place in the center of world affairs. That illusion lasted until the early 19th century when the Qing Dynasty (c. 1644–1912), nominally dominated by ethnic Manchus, was forced into humiliating and unequal treaties with Britain as a result of the Opium Wars.

Between the First Opium War (1839–1842) and the Communist Takeover of China (1949), the Chinese suffered from political and cultural dominance by the British. This largely caused the Taiping Rebellion (1850–1864), led by a Chinese Christian convert, that probably killed as many people as WWI. Chinese weakness enticed the Japanese to invade in 1894 and their inability to control the Korean Peninsula led to a Japanese annexation of Korea in 1910. As the Japanese grew more militaristic and racist, they increasingly brutalized the people in any foreign territory under their control, invaded Manchuria in 1931, and in 1937 forced themselves into Nanking, the horror which is encapsulated in the title of Iris Chang's 1991 classic *The Rape of Nanking.*

We should be aware of China's humiliations, because that history is at the front of Chinese historical education. In his book, *Everything Under the Heavens: How the Past Helps Shape China's Push for Global Power* (2017), Howard W. French writes:

> In its most familiar form, the narrative of the demise of the Chinese world order is the story of rampaging Western Imperialism's triumphant march into East Asia. In its textbooks and in its nationalist propaganda, China itself has styled the one-hundred-year period during which the modern world was built as its Century of Humiliation. . . . (p. 9)

Control of the Pacific Rim and the South China Sea, and especially the prostration of Japan, is key to the Communist Party's sense of political rebirth. Please remember that China is surrounded by examples of successful Asian democracies that are close with the United States.

When one considers how much American foreign policy was focused on a little impoverished island like Cuba, it becomes clear that the Chinese consider themselves besieged by Asian democracies that hold American ties; the Chinese south is surrounded by Japan, South Korea, Taiwan, and the Philippines. Even the Vietnamese prefer American connections. The core mission of the Chinese Communist Party is to develop and extend China's global political influence, especially in the Pacific.

Even the best western analysts tend to misunderstand the nature of modern China, partially because of a false belief that the Communist power structure there will inevitably collapse as did the Soviet Union in 1991. Or, even worse, the West treats the Chinese power structure as somehow more benign than the Soviet Union. Some Western analysts likely even believe that a single party state with top-down control of the economy might be a necessary phase for a developing country like China. These conceits are delusions.

In 2017, the 19th National Congress of the Communist Party of China took place. At that congress, over two thousand communist patsies (aka delegates) voted with meek unanimity to give "President" Xi Jinping not just dictatorial powers of China, but his own "school of thought." The latter act turned Jinping into the political equivalent of Mao Zedong (a great compliment in that crowd). Jinping, like Mao before him, wields the power of a Stalin.

What does it mean to be the heir to Mao? In the words of Mao's modern biographers, Jung Chang and Jon Halliday, "Mao's ultimate ambition was to dominate the world" (p. 553), and he planned to do this through the development of a nuclear weapons program. Even those with a casual acquaintance to history know that Mao instituted the Great Leap Forward (1958–1962) and with it the deadliest idea of the Twentieth Century: the so-called "backyard steel mill." Mao hoped to catch up to the West by having the peasants make a little steel in their backyards in the afternoon after collecting the harvest.

Communist bureaucrats competed with each other to make the most steel in their regions, and after a couple of years of this, the harvest of actual food was neglected. The "steel mills" produced almost nothing but worthless pig iron, and some estimates have it that 60 million Chinese died.

Part of the reason so many died was because Mao refused to redirect funds from his nuclear weapons program to alleviate the famine. The famine did not trouble Mao for the same reason that he welcomed the idea of nuclear war:China had more people than anyone else and could afford to lose huge percentages of its population. The plan for global conquest was what mattered, as Chang and Halliday write:

> It was for the sake of this world ambition that Mao had embarked on hair-raising risks in the nuclear field. The most scary of these came on 27 October, 1966, when a missile armed with an atomic warhead was fired 800 km across northwest China, over sizable towns—the only such test ever undertaken by any nation on Earth, and with a missile known to be far from accurate. . . . Three days beforehand, Mao told the man in charge to proceed, saying that he was prepared for the test to fail (p. 553).

Mao and the world got lucky with that 1966 shot; the test somehow managed to work, but the attitude of ideology-before-human-beings still dominates. This is not unique to China's history. In 1931, Joseph Stalin cited Russia's past humiliations as a reason to forcibly industrialize the Soviet Union. "To slacken the tempo would mean falling behind. And those who fall behind get beaten." The Pakistani Prime Minister Zulfikar Ali Bhutto (1928–1979) memorably stated, "We will eat grass . . . but will get [an atom bomb] . . . we have no choice." It's also the guiding philosophy of both North Korea and Iran; it's a philosophy best describe as "nuclear weapons and global political influence at any cost to the people."

What does it mean to be the heir to Deng Xiaoping (1904–1997)? After the death of Mao in 1976, Deng Xiaoping took power in 1978 and brought with him a concept of economic reform. What occurred next causes the most confusion among Western historians and political analysts. Xiaoping cited Vladimir Lenin's 1921 *New Economic Policy* (NEP) as the precedent for his policies. After the 1917 Bolshevik Revolution, Lenin and the Communist Party had to fight a Civil War against counter-revolutionary forces. Lenin won, but economic stagnation nearly ruined the country and Lenin allowed farmers to sell their grain on the open market (capitalism) as a way of trying to revive Russia's economy.

In the abstract of a 2018 paper for a foreign policy journal, Wei Xiaping states that ". . . the guiding principle of [Deng's] policy was almost the same" as the NEP. Xiaoping never disagreed with the global ambitions of Mao; he disagreed with the tactics. The best tactic to revive China and make her a dominant communist hegemon was to create, as Lenin briefly did, a state-dominated capitalist economy that could create enough wealth to further

China's military plans. When the Soviet Union collapsed, Xiaoping's modern biographer, Ezra F. Vogel wrote this of Xiaoping's reaction:

> In attempting to explain what had gone wrong in the Soviet Union, Deng asserted that the Soviet Union had failed to institute economic reforms in a timely manner and that the top Soviet leaders had not firmly supported the Communist Party. Instead, Soviet leaders had become caught up in an arms race with the United States, a contest that had led to wasteful spending that did not improve the lives of ordinary people" (p. 658).

Xi Jinping's "school of thought" reaffirms that China should be the world's dominant power, that Communist ideology should be supreme, and that the best means to accomplish this is not through a direct military confrontation with the West, but through rapid economic development that is guided from the top down by a single party state. The welfare of the people is important only so far as it prevents revolutions and supports the Party's global military and economic ambitions.

Between 1492 and 1750, a variety of historical forces reshaped Western Europe, and Great Britain in particular, into an industrialized imperial force. This happened naturally and in a bottom-up manner in the West, but it forced areas of the world outside of the West to try and direct "Westernization" from the top down. Russia's Czar Peter the Great (1672–1725) was the first autocrat to realize that Westernization was not an option. Peter forced Western style science and engineering on Russia, but did not adopt any of the democratic institutions of the West. Ever since Peter, this has been the autocrat's dream: to have the military, economic, social, and political power of the West without any Western democratic reforms.

Yet, a push for power without reform is always dangerous to the world because democratic institutions that are participated in by free peoples put a check on the worst power-grabbing impulses. A couple of examples of this will suffice to make the point and to connect the coronavirus to China.

In 1853, Commodore Matthew Perry was sent by President Millard Fillmore to force Japan into the global trade network. The Japanese had sequestered themselves from the world in the 17th century, when Portuguese missionaries threated Japan's feudal structure. As a result, the Japanese remained stuck with feudal military technologies and could do nothing but row their boats out to confront Perry's steamships. The Japanese submitted to American demands to trade whale oil and coal, but in 1868 made it a national priority to militarize and become a global power.

Unfortunately, the Japanese decided that the way to gain international respect was to militarize, invade other countries, and treat them with racist disdain. The Chinese and Koreans suffered the most from Japanese policy, but on December 7, 1941, the United States became suddenly aware that Japan's rapid industrialization, uncoupled from real democratic accountability, was the world's problem.

Likewise, when the Soviet Union pushed to create thermonuclear weapons after the Second World War, they did so on the cheap and without regard to the effect that the diversion of funds had on the people. Both the Soviet space program and the Soviet nuclear power program were derived from the arms race, and in both cases the Soviets pushed engineers to build faster and cheaper. Safety regulations became an afterthought. Institutions of internal control would only divert from the mission and no free press existed to draw attention to the dangers. Soviet ideology led to the 1986 Chernobyl meltdown, and the world realized, suddenly, the dangers that unaccountable governments with global ambitions pose to the world.

The Chinese government cares nothing for the health of their own citizens, except to the extent that the citizens help to develop the aims of the communist party. China's government will be untroubled by the staggering effects that COVID-19 has inflicted upon the globe; this only helps their ambitions. Mao believed that the sheer size of China's population would allow them to survive global catastrophes more effectively than Western societies where the populations were hampered by such things as cheap and effective birth control.

COVID-19 almost certainly evolved in one the "wet markets" in Wuhan China. The conditions of these markets could not occur in American society because of the existence of health and safety standards and because free people would feel comfortable reporting to their government. Health and safety standards are no more the priority of the modern Chinese Communist Party than were the nuclear safety standards in the Soviet Union in 1986. COVID-19 is China's Chernobyl.

What is to be done? In the aftermath of the Second World War, the United States led the development of the United Nations and Eleanor Roosevelt led the creation of the Universal Declaration of Human Rights that became the founding document of that international body. At the same time, both Japan and Nazi Germany were reformed into stable democracies. Two nations who had committed some of history's most ghastly atrocities are, in 2020, highly functioning democracies with impressive economies. Not too long ago, the Western powers understood this: democratic institutions that respected the rights and freedoms of the people were the answer to the world's challenges.

It still is the answer. The Chinese government needs to be held accountable by the world's democracies. China needs to face a united front of democratic institutions that demand A. that China submit to health and safety inspections by outside entities and B. that China institute democratic reforms. If the Communist Party does not submit to these reforms they must face trade sanctions and global alienation, and the free peoples of the world must understand that any market deprivations these cause are worth the price, lest another random virus be released upon the world in the near future.

Yes, this is what history looks like, and it's time for it, finally, to end.

Conclusion

One would think that ethics, being the most practical branch of philosophy, would be taught in elementary and high schools. Everyone encounters ethical decisions daily, and ethical dilemmas, big and small, feature in daily life. In addition to being practical, no other subject challenges a student to think in novel ways and to make use of analogical thinking like an ethical case does. Ethical questions in themselves then require that an ethicist develop an understanding of content in order to make the best choice.

KEY IDEAS AND CLASSROOM APPLICATION

- Ethical cases provide an interesting entry point into analogical thinking. Ethical thinking is dependent upon the creation of hypothetical "thought experiments" and, therefore, is perhaps the subject best suited to this book's subject.
- Since the 19th century, ethical reasoning has been made to mimic algebra. Logicians typically developed "truth tables" that operate on a binary process. The binary approach to ethics makes it difficult to analyze subjects where a slow pace of change occurs.
- When using an ethical approach to analyze history, the only reasonable conclusion is that inclusive (democratic) governments that respect basic freedoms operate more effectively than governments that act in an oppressive and unaccountable manner.

Chapter Eight

Meta-Mathematics and Meta-Language

Mathematics can be, and probably initially should be, studied without an understanding of its historical development. Real value exists in the process of learning how to solve linear equations, use existing information as a base for finding hidden information, and solve quadratics. Mathematics is, emphatically, useful in a practical way and that is especially true when one studies and applies statistics and informatics. But at some point, mathematics butts up against metaphysical boundaries, and that's where the best thought experiments develop; only by studying the history of math can those boundaries become visible.

Defining the term "mathematics" is a problem since the first idea that presents itself is to call "mathematics" a symbology that stands for something. A line in the sand might stand for a single tree, but in abstract mathematics the symbols do not necessarily stand in for something concrete. Mathematics might be defined then as "the manipulation of symbols used for the purpose of understanding phenomena both real and developed only in the mind." This is vague, but it is more likely that mathematics is used to impose a sense of order on the chaos of the universe than it is to uncover truths planted in the universe *a priori*.

The history of mathematics, then, is analogous to the history of language; both could only develop as a product of human evolution and the development of the human mind. Although the numbers 0 through 9 are now ubiquitous, this numerical system developed over the course of centuries in India and culminated with the creation of the number 0 about 500 CE. From there, those numerals traveled to the Arabic/Islamic world and were developed by philosophers into algebra and trigonometry.

105

Although some attempts were made, particularly by the Pope of the year 1000, Sylvester II, to bring these nubile symbols to Christendom, the first person to succeed was Fibonacci (b.1170), and not until the late 13th century. At the time, the only other major "mathematical" system consisted of Roman numerals, and they were too stiff to compete with 0–9, which proved to be more effective for banking. About the same time this transference occurred, new applications for these numbers were noticed by Islamic mathematicians, who developed trigonometry.

Here is where several different ideas converged at once. In the 16th century Renee Descartes (1596–1650) created the well-known X–Y (or Cartesian) graph. This happened to be the era when cannon technology, itself a synthesis of medieval church bells and Chinese gunpowder, became the weapon of choice for armies on the besieging side. Cannonballs inaugurated physics because the measurement of their trajectory could be determined mathematically and applied practically to such important work as knocking down castle walls.

In the 17th century, Newton realized that the arc of a cannonball is a partial orbit, and the same forces that shaped the trajectory of a cannonball into a parabola also kept the planets spinning around the sun. In turn, this realization required the creation of the Inverse Square Law which states that the further away that an object gets from the source of the gravity, the weaker the gravitational pull becomes.

Now, plot some cannonballs on a Cartesian graph and one can determine the axis of symmetry and vertex using various formulas, including the quadratic. At some point, however, those little cannonballs became abstract and could stand not just for real cannonballs but data points. By plotting little points on the graph, it became possible to keep track of trends within evidence. Statisticians now keep track of inflation rates using the same techniques, only with different input values (sometimes functions) than those physicists use to predict and describe the arc of a cannonball.

This brings up a question: are interest rates like cannonball arcs or is the analogy is being forced because once humans found a means of understanding one thing, they tried to use it to understand a lot of things? Is it useful to develop data points and graphs by inputting functions into mini-cannonballs and then moving those cannonballs around to reflect not the effect of gravity, but of something even more mysterious, like consumer confidence?

It is fascinating to consider that, with the right information in place, one can use -B over 2A (B and A referencing the order of terms in an equation) as a way of discovering the vertex for both a cannonball arc and for something like consumer confidence. Is it the case that Newton discovered a specific use for a general concept, meaning that he discovered a means of plotting input and output values that just happened to involve gravity and ball trajectory? This would mean his great contribution was not in practical physics, but in the discovery that information of any kind could be plotted on a graph and developed into a means of understanding patterns in information.

Most people look at Cartesian graphs that contain all kinds of different varieties of information without connecting the data points to cannonballs. This is much like how people will stare at clocks and watches their whole lives and never realize the connection between the clock and the ruler. Yet these are profound connections and insights in terms of understanding metaphysics.

Likewise, people unfamiliar with trigonometry might wonder why an entire branch of mathematics focuses on one shape. How many triangles does the average person encounter in her life anyway? The point of trigonometry, however, is that one creates the triangles on a Cartesian plane in order to then use either the Pythagorean theorem or the six trigonometric functions to determine the numerical precisions of objects in motion. Trigonometry imposes a sense of understanding on the functions of the universe. Is this an arbitrary imposition, in the same way that spoken languages are arbitrary, or is there something special about the triangle?

The fact is that the latter answer could be, and probably is, true, but not because of any mystical reason. The triangle simply makes itself apparent when a mathematician starts drawing linear X and Y lines. The same results could be achieved using other shapes, but drawing rectangles on a Cartesian plane is more complicated than drawing triangles. Likewise, Relativity Theory could have been based on the speed of sound rather than the speed of light, but this would have limited its descriptive powers to objects moving more slowly than the speed of sound.

Cannonballs and triangles are the specific examples that allowed mathematicians to uncover the general principles. Something similar happened when Einstein developed first the Special Theory of Relativity and then the General Theory of Relativity. This general process would indicate that the human mind, from the beginning of civilization, continues to find uses that it was pre-adapted for and does so through the consistent use of analogies. When someone develops a specific understanding for one phenomenon it later becomes useful for developing a general understanding for greater levels of phenomena.

In some ways, Geometry functions like theology. Both begin with statements that are taken to be true and the creativity comes from developing a logical structure underneath the statement itself. Philosophy, in contrast, begins with questions and the logic is built underneath a conclusion. The concept of the Geometric Proof can actually be explained using language. Students might be asked to find a way to make this statement true:

Veterinarians are people doctors.

A literal interpretation of this statement makes no sense, but through reasoning and dialogue, one could make the statement true. If people suffer emotional trauma because a beloved pet is sick, then when a veterinarian treats the physical ailment of the pet it is the case, by proxy, that the emotional trauma of the pet owner can also be healed.

These are not just word games. If one proves that veterinarians are people doctors in this way, then the following statement can also be made true after, say, a mother is diagnosed with breast cancer:

That family has breast cancer.

Again, a literal interpretation of this would not make sense but one can realize that the meaning is that if the mother develops breast cancer then this creates hardships and emotional trauma that affect the entire family. What's the significance of this new understanding? Well, in many cases, government employees are given sick days, only a certain number of which can be used for "family" sick days. A changing conception of the way in which cancer affects the entire family might change that policy and erase the distinction between a family and a personal sick day. Here is another phrase that has become a commonplace sentiment:

That couple is pregnant.

This is actually a fairly common statement, and people pretty quickly understood that the meaning of it is that the husband and wife are engaged in a shared process and responsibility. It is not hard to discern that meaning. Now, the issue with a consciousness-raising statement like this is that it could possibly create a misleading notion pregnancy. Single women often become pregnant and so, clearly, pregnancy is not based upon a shared relationship and responsibility in all circumstances, so "that couple is pregnant" effectively alters the meaning of the word pregnancy.

Consider this, though, if we agree that couples get pregnant then it would mean that couples should both receive benefits for a childcare leave from work. It would also mean that a single mother should receive the same kind of leave, plus extra money because, if her male partner is not involved in the raising of the child, then his section of the benefits remain unused and should therefore be passed on to the mother. If that sounds strange, then consider that because the "father" is not using his child-leave benefits then those benefits are effectively advantaging some employer somewhere because the employer is not having to lose the father's labor.

Finding novel ways to make a geometric statement true is not much different from the process of making statements in language true using novel forms of thought. In both cases, however, the reinterpretation of a statement to create a novel proof can alter the rest of the logic connected to it. It is sort of like how a novel has actions that are connected to other actions, so editing becomes difficult if removing a chapter takes out the logic behind the motivation of the characters in a later chapter. Sometimes changing a meaning or connection between meanings, alters the entire narrative connected to the original.

To use one more example, let's look at this phrase:

Black lives matter.

Those who take offense at the phrase usually assume it contains another word, which would make it read, "Black lives matter *more*." If one reads it that way, then the counter is "all lives matter," because that phrase is more inclusive. However, the implied notion in "Black lives matter," is that society somehow does not understand or agree with the point that Black lives actually do matter, and so the statement needs to be made. To disagree with "Black lives matter" is to disagree with the underlying assumption that society does not value Black lives. Therefore, to say "all lives matter" is to effectively discount the idea that an underlying inequality exists.

This makes it reasonable to categorize "Black lives matter" with signs that prohibit behavior. When one encounters a "No Smoking" sign, then the underlying assumption is that the sign is there because there is a reasonable chance that someone might try to smoke in that space. If one encounters a sign that reads "No geese on a leash allowed in this establishment," then one might ask, "When was this a problem?" The nature of the statements in the case of both "No Smoking" and "Black lives matter" is that some problem exists that needs to be addressed. If one does not see the problem, then the statement takes on a different connotation.

To use another analogy, if someone in authority says, "Look, I'm in charge here," the underlying assumption of the statement is that there is some question about who is in charge. Thus, a statement intended to enhance someone's authority can actually undermine it because the assumption speaks more loudly than the statement.

These kinds of activities, like asking students to analyze a clock and a ruler, have the effect of developing more creative variations of thought and analysis. These are ways to develop an intrinsic interest in students that, in turn, can enhance the students' ability to absorb content and develop skills. This method effectively blends all the content areas into a single body of knowledge, while also creative an effective method for understanding and teaching this approach to knowledge.

KEY IDEAS AND CLASSROOM APPLICATIONS

- Studying the history of mathematics leads to the discovery of meta-questions about the boundaries of mathematical application. Those questions are framed around thought experiments and can be useful ways to engage students.
- Coordinates on a Cartesian graph originated with the study of cannonball trajectory which leads to the question of whether are cannonball analogies are useful for understanding other forms of information, or if the study of cannonball trajectory was just the first example of how a function on a graph works.
- Mathematics and language are analogous in many ways and so the same processes that form mathematical understanding can also be used to develop meaning with words.

Conclusion

Thought experiments depend upon the development of proper hypotheticals that take reality into account and employ the closest analogies for purposes of understanding. Though many thought experiments have become famous, they tend to be viewed by scientists as interesting for developing explanatory clarity, but not particularly useful for actually "doing" science. The process remains scattershot—occasionally employed, but not developed to its full potential.

The purpose of this book was not just to create a historical background for thought experiments, but to show their use in clarifying models involving time, psychology, ethics, and even history. My hope is also that this book will encourage caution in anyone who hopes to develop a thought experiment in any field of study. Thought experiments are delicate, and their parameters can easily be torn down when new facts are discovered or a slight difference is found between the thought experiment and its real-world analog. Improper thought experiments can lead to the wrong type of decision making, particularly in politics and ethics.

Generally speaking, bad decisions get made because the thought processes behind the decisions remain connected to some long-standing historical process that traps someone's thinking. Most of the time, people cannot see how their thinking is connected to these historically-created structures. We feel guilty for violating norms created thousands of years ago for other places and peoples, yet cannot see that those norms might need to shift.

A woman in Afghanistan, for example, might feel just as guilty for leaving the house without her burka as a homosexual male would have felt in conservative Christian Ireland during the 1950s. Thought experiments help to update the ethical norms with the times; they develop clarity and can do real good.

Mostly, however, the thought experiment reaches its full potential as a teaching method. The teacher can express an old thought experiment, create a new one, or ask students to create them. The creation of thought experiments is engaging and useful, and in the process of doing so, students will find that they must master certain forms of content in order to develop the parameters of thought experiments.

Given their importance in the history of ideas, it would seem that thought experiments would be given a great place of importance as a discrete intellectual category. The classroom potential for a curriculum based on thought experiments is vast. Even in this age of research and wealth there is a place for experiments created out of pure thought.

References

Arthur, Benjamin. (2015). *The Magic of Math: Solving for X and Figuring Out Why.* New York: Basic Books.

Asimov, Isaac. (1950) *I, Robot.* New York: The Gnome Press.

Coates, Ta-Nehisi. (2015). *Between the World and Me.* New York: Penguin Books.

Chang, Iris. (1991). *The Rape of Nanking: The Forgotten Holocaust of WWII.* New York: Basic Books.

Chang, Jung, and Jon Halladay, Jon (2005). *The Unknown Story of Mao.* New York: Anchor Books.

Criado-Perez, Caroline. (2019). *Invisible Women: Data Bias in a World Designed for Men.* New York: Henry N. Abrams.

Free Solo. (2018). National Geographic Films.

French, Howard W. (2017). *Everything Under the Heavens: How the Past Helps Shape China's Push for Global Power.* New York: Alfred A. Knopf.

Gleick, James. (2016). *Time Travel: A History.* New York: Pantheon.

Gribbin, John. (2017). *Einstein's Masterwork: 1915 and the General Theory of Relativity.* New York/London: Pegasus Books.

Kline, Morris. (Reprint: 1985). *Mathematics for the Nonmathematician.* New York: Dover Publications.

Morrison, Toni. (1977). *Song of Solomon.* New York: Alfred A. Knopf.

Morrison, Toni. (1987). *Beloved.* New York: Alfred A. Knopf.

Ohlson, Kristin. (2011)."The End of Morality." Discover Magazine.

Pinker, Steven. (2018). *Enlightenment Now: The Case for Reason, Science, Humanism, and Progress.* New York: Penguin Books.

Vogel, Ezra F. (2011). *Deng Xiaoping And the Transformation of China.* Cambridge: The Belknap Press of Harvard University Press.

WEB REFERENCES

Davies, Paul. (2007)."The Flexi-Laws of Physics." New Scientist. https://www.new-scientist.com/article/mg19426101-300-the-flexi-laws-of-physics/.

The Declaration of Sentiments (1848). https://www.britannica.com/event/Declaration-of-Sentiments.

Lincoln, Abraham. (1858). https://www.goodreads.com/quotes/602394-it-is-the-eternal-struggle-between-these-two-principles.

Marx, Karl, and Friedrich Engels. (1848). *The Manifesto of the Communist Party.* https://www.marxists.org/archive/marx/works/1848/communist-manifesto/.

Stalin on Rapid Industrialization. Speech to Industrial Managers. February 1931. https://academic.shu.edu/russianhistory/index.php/Stalin_on_Rapid_Industrialization.

Xiaoping, Wei. (2018). "Lenin's NEP and Deng Xiaoping's Economic Reform." In *The Palgrave Handbook of Leninist Political Philosophy*, pp. 531-548. https://link.springer.com/chapter/10.1057/978-1-137-51650-3_18.